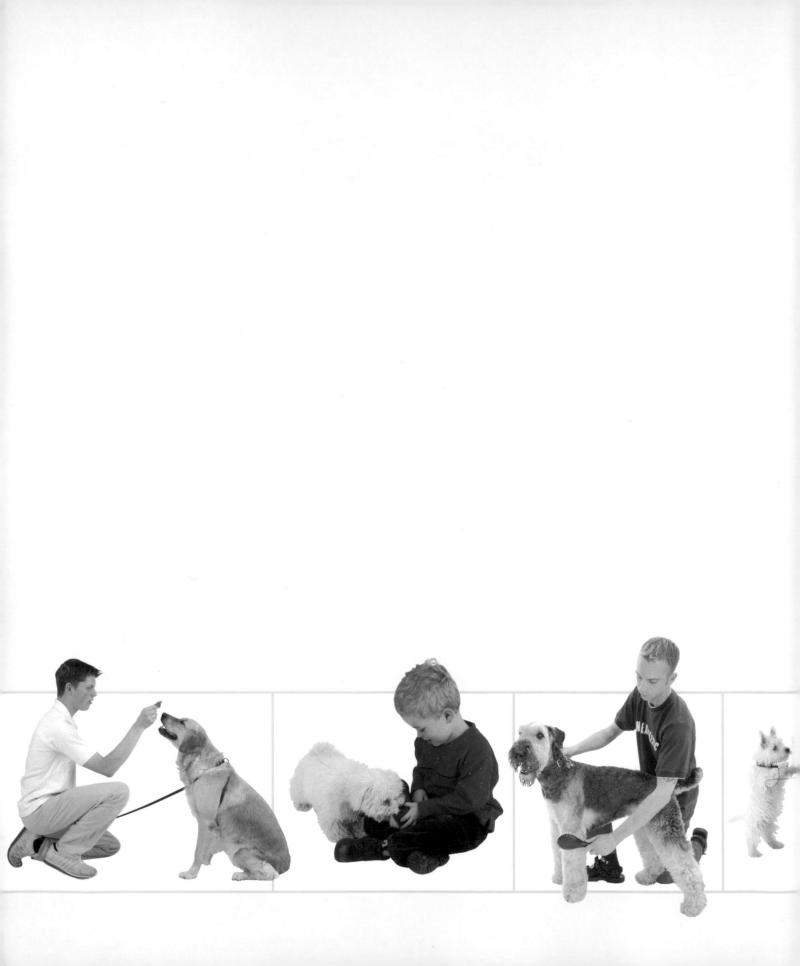

Breaking Bad Habits
in
DOGS

Breaking Bad Habits

in

DOGS

Learn to gain the obedience and trust of
your dog by understanding the way
dogs think and behave

Colin Tennant

BARRON'S

► Notes on Using This Book

This book sets out to explain what goes on inside a dog's mind and to make sense of why dogs behave as they do, particularly why they appear to behave badly (to our way of thinking). It also gives advice on training exercises and other measures that can be used to remedy bad behavior. Used sensibly, the programs described in this book are quite safe, but readers must be aware that some dogs are powerful animals that may on occasion behave unpredictably. Dogs that display characteristics such as aggression should always be approached with caution; if in doubt, seek the advice of a qualified dog trainer or behavior practitioner first.

The information and recommendations in this book are given without any guarantees on behalf of the author and publisher, who disclaim any liability with the use of this material.

► Readers will see that in this book I sometimes recommend that a problem dog should be referred to a dog trainer or a canine behaviorist. Both professionals should have a clear understanding of canine psychology and the reasons why some dogs behave badly. However, do be aware that few behaviorists—even academically qualified ones—can train dogs to a high standard. This is something that you should know before you seek help.

When following the advice given in each chapter, readers should decide which training measures to use, bearing in mind their circumstances and the age and breed of the dog in question. In some cases, it would not be practical to use all the methods described at the same time.

First edition for the United States and Canada published in 2003 by Barron's Educational Series, Inc.

First published in 2002 by Interpet Publishing
© Copyright 2002 by Interpet Publishing

All rights reserved

All inquiries should be addressed to:
Barron's Educational Series, Inc.
250 Wireless Boulevard
Hauppauge, NY 11788
http://www.barronseduc.com

International Standard Book No.: 0-7641-2235-5

Library of Congress Catalog Card No.: 2001099032

Printed in Hong Kong
9 8 7 6 5

► The Author

Colin Tennant is Britain's leading expert in dog behavior and obedience training. He operates a canine behavior center providing advice and assistance for owners of dogs of all breeds. In 1975, he served in the Cheshire Police Dog Section and is Home Office-qualified as a police dog handler. Colin began his career in canine behavior and obedience training at the Asoka Training School in Manchester. In the early 1980s, he founded the London Dog Training Group, specializing in one-to-one training for problem dogs.

Colin has trained animals for more than 100 television programs and has made several instructional videos dealing with training problems as well as the care of cats and other pets. He lectures around the world and is a frequent contributor to national newspapers and magazines. He is employed as a consultant by the media and has provided expert advice on dog behavior and training to the BBC and other national TV networks as well as to radio programs and filmmakers. He is Chairman of the Canine and Feline Behaviour Association based in Great Britain and senior pet behavior practitioner working at his Canine and Feline Behaviour Centre situated in Hertfordshire.

▶ Contents

▶Introduction

Origins of the Dog

The dog curled up by your feet has been man's faithful companion for thousands of years. Originally domesticated from its wild cousins, the dog is now one of the world's most popular pets, with millions sharing our homes. We find many of their characteristics familiar and lovable, but we often fail to appreciate the natural inheritance that they carry with them (the characteristics that make them dogs). We tend to demand that all pets we domesticate should fit in with our lifestyle. To understand dogs' behavior, it helps to know something about their history and innate nature.

The Early History of Dogs

Archaeological excavations have revealed that dogs have lived around man for perhaps as long as a hundred thousand years. The ancient Egyptians kept dogs for many purposes; they worshipped the jackal-headed god Anubis, and dogs were often buried next to their masters, which indicates how greatly the Egyptians respected their dogs. The Ancient Greeks, Chinese, and Romans also kept and trained dogs and afforded them great status in their respective societies. One famous Japanese emperor owned 100,000 dogs that all enjoyed royal protection.

Over time, man has bred dogs selectively to enhance those canine abilities of which he has need and to harness the instincts he finds most useful. For example, Collies have far better herding instincts than any wolf and German Shepherds more confidence and guarding/shepherding ability combined. The sighthounds are swifter than a wolf. Mastiffs were bred for their strength and fighting qualities, both against men and animals.

More than 400 breeds exist worldwide, and each year more are added to the list. While looking at them, you may wonder what our ancestors were trying to achieve with their selective breeding. A Chihuahua, for instance, isn't suited to herding or guarding for it weighs no more than three or four pounds (2 kg). No, the Chihuahua, the smallest breed

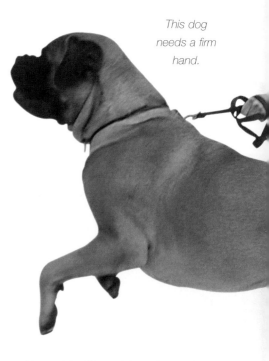

This dog needs a firm hand.

Left: The German Shepherd is an extremely versatile working dog as well as being one of our most popular pets.

Above: *Mastiffs are big and powerful dogs that have for centuries been bred by man as fighting dogs, both for use in battle and when hunting wild animals. Despite their fierce appearance, they have quite placid temperaments.*

in the world, was bred purely for human fancy—providing companionship and religious significance. The Pekingese is a similar example.

Working Breeds

The shepherding and retrieving breeds are without doubt the most malleable dogs that respond to human training and so are the ones most commonly found working alongside man. The dogs that actually work alongside

Right: Toy dogs are particularly affectionate and faithful companion animals. Despite their small size, they can be very effective guard dogs.

If not properly trained, a Mastiff may prove difficult to handle when taken for a walk.

Companionship

Most dogs are acquired as family pets. Evidence from the Society for Companion Animal Studies at Glasgow and Cambridge Universities clearly shows that people live longer and lead more contented lives when they own a dog. The elderly and single people benefit greatly from owning a dog: it helps them to meet other people on walks, keeps them fit, and provides a rewarding source of companionship. As society becomes more stressful, dogs and other pets will no doubt continue to satisfy important social and psychological needs for many people. However, is this necessarily good for the pets? We shall see.

Below right: For people who live alone, dogs can be a lifeline, providing affection and friendship in an otherwise empty house. Their company can even have beneficial health effects, helping to counter depression and speeding up the time it takes to recover from an illness.

man in the modern world include police dogs, guide dogs, sheepdogs, assistance dogs, and others. The essential role that dogs now play in society is demonstrated admirably by the sniffer dog. Many a drug courier's face drops at the sight of the approaching sniffer dog in an airport lounge.

Left: Appearances can be deceptive—the Labrador looks a picture of domestication, but deep down inside there beats the heart of a wild animal.

strange, nondoggy behavior and peculiar environment. Getting along together is a two-way process.

If you truly understand your dog and respect him, you will be fascinated rather than let down when your dog behaves like a wolf. So let's now examine some examples of dog/wolf behavior that we can all recognize.

Sniffing and Rolling

Dogs sniff each other, humans, and urine and feces deposited by other dogs and animals. Why? Because that's their messaging system, the equivalent in many

Domestic Problems

Despite their value in the home, too many people choose dogs that are unsuitable for their homes and lifestyles. It must be remembered that a pet dog is in essence a wolf in Labrador's (or any other breed's) clothing. Man has done a good job of disguising the real wolf through breeding so that we can no longer see the wild animal lurking inside our dogs. Well, we don't see it until the dog begins to behave badly or (as I would say) like its cousin the wolf.

This self-deception is the crux of many of the behavioral problems that I encounter and that will be featured in this book. Dogs know what they are; most owners don't. It can take some time and many consultations before they realize that they have willingly been breeding, loving, and caring for a wolf in their home.

Man's Best Friend

Most people take dogs for granted. They expect that they will be loyal, obedient, friendly, sociable and dependable friends who attend to our every word and desire. When we read about someone being bitten by a dog, we recoil in disbelief and assume that this is an unusual occurrence. The fact is that if (as we often do) we expect dogs to be what they are not, then we will be disappointed when they behave badly or unsociably. Or—if you wish—like a dog.

Equally, dogs are bound to feel fed up when we leave them at home alone while we enjoy an evening out. They are pack animals, not solitary creatures. The dog may not understand our reasons, but they do learn to adapt to our ways of your eyes checking a sign or an advertisement in a newspaper. It advertises their presence. Scent is also important in the hunt for food.

Food equals survival, and so most animals have powerful instincts in this crucial department. Until taught differently, they will gladly take any food they sniff out or see from a dog bowl or the street or from your coffee table. Dogs are predators and scavengers, and finding free food is a slice

Above: By nature dogs are pack animals like their wolf ancestors. It is not surprising that they look out of sorts when forced to spend long periods of time on their own in the house.

Above right: Where food is concerned, dogs instinctively always look for an opportunity. They must be trained to distinguish between your table and their own food bowl.

Left: When dogs meet, they often circle one another, sniffing the anal and genital areas. They use scent as a way of gathering information about the world.

of luck not to be ignored. Some dog instincts are hard to accept. Dogs like rolling in animal manure to mask their own smell—much to the disgust of most owners. They also mark dead prey by rolling and impregnating their own scent on the carcass, thereby laying claim to it. They do it instinctively, but we see it as a dirty habit.

Pack Rules

Many dogs will strive to dominate any other dogs or humans with whom they come into contact by body language and/or growling, biting, or aggressive physical bullying. If you understand this wolflike behavior, you will be better able to train, control, and respect your dog. Remember, these instincts have helped the wolf to become one of the most successful species in the world.

Dogs are hunters, so it's normal for them to chase a moving object, whether it's a jogger, a cat, or a squirrel. Larger dogs may knock over valuable household ornaments or even jump up and knock us over in their enthusiasm to greet us upon our return, just as they would greet fellow pack members returning from the hunt. However, in the wolf pack, other dogs stand conveniently on four legs and at muzzle level, where they can be licked without jumping up. With humans, it's a different story.

Below: During the formative stages of puppyhood, the dog is becoming part of the family pack.

Pack Behavior

Dogs love digging in soft soil or sand, and they enjoy burying bones or toys; this is their way of saving food for a rainy day. They do not intentionally mean to damage our beautiful lawns. They simply cannot see any harm in this instinctive action. Dogs, particularly males, also mark territory through urination and scent gland secretions; this is the dog's way of marking his hunting areas to secure his food supply and of letting other dogs know of his presence.

When you return home from shopping, watch your dog's reactions. Your dog will sniff you all over with excitement because you have many scents on your clothes and shopping items. He will act like a puppy wolf, excitedly welcoming the adult wolves back from a hunting trip. In fact, domesticated dogs retain juvenile characteristics all their adult lives as a consequence of their domestication.

Dogs often lick us with great enthusiasm. They particularly like our faces, though the feeling is not always mutual! This is the dog's method of reinforcing body contact with the pack and showing deference to higher-ranking pack members. Puppies lick to request a mouthful of regurgitated meat.

If not restrained, dogs will wander over great distances. They like meeting and investigating other dogs; sniffing the genitals and the anuses of other dogs is a great source of information and a

Above: Domestic dogs have inherited the wolf's innate awareness of the dynamics of pack behavior. Pack animals have to learn to fit into a pack hierarchy, and this explains why many pet dogs seek to dominate other dogs with which they come into contact through aggressive displays.

It's natural for dogs to bark as a warning or a call for help, but persistent barking is a nuisance that can ruin the enjoyment of owning a dog.

Below: *This juxtaposition of pictures is revealing—the domestic dog crouching, ready to play behind its toy, and the wolf waiting alertly in the snow look remarkably similar. Much of the behavior of a dog is influenced by its wolflike instincts.*

display of politeness. Dogs also like using their voices and may bark, howl, or yap as an expression of their mood or excitement. Wolves do all these things too, with the exception of barking, which is a rarely used part of their vocabulary.

It must be appreciated that these behaviors are normal, though they may not always be appropriate to our circumstances. In fact, behavioral problems are very much specific to circumstances. For example, a dog that chases squirrels in the country is probably not a problem dog for its owner, but a dog doing the same thing in a busy city park may be considered a danger by its owner because of the distress it causes to other park users and the likelihood of its running into the road while in pursuit of its quarry.

Above: *Dogs—and wolves—are vocal creatures. Dogs use their voices to communicate with other canines. Wolves use vocal signals to warn of danger and to summon other pack members.*

Above: *Instinctively, dogs are hunters— the desire to chase other animals is something that is born within them.*

Below 1: Children can benefit greatly from the pleasure a playing with a well-behaved pet. But they, like dogs, need to learn the rules.

Below 2: The dog must be taught to defer to human pack members.

Above 3: Dogs do not generally view young children as high ranking. Obedience training helps that process.

1

2

3

Dominance

I do not adopt a rigid view of dominant dogs. Dogs vary so immensely in character, temperament, and behavior that hard-and-fast rules do not apply. My experience of dealing with many thousands of badly behaved dogs has taught me that trying to prejudge their behavior is unsuccessful in terms of rehabilitation or training.

I follow the safe route in all dog training and when acting to modify unacceptable dog behavior. If you follow my rules, then ideally the dog will stop displaying excessive dominance; at the very least, the behavior should be altered to a manageable level. Wolves naturally and constantly suppress one another and we as humans need to suppress our dogs' natural inclination to try to dominate us.

Dog Training and Behavior

Many bad behaviors in dogs can be altered or prevented by obedience training and the methods described in this book. This is why it's so important to set the ground rules when a new puppy or adult dog arrives. Whether you train using books, videos, a training club, or a private instructor, obedience is a necessity and a continuing process throughout the dog's life. Dog training is not dissimilar to human learning—it should continue from birth to death and be constantly reinforced.

The bottom line with dogs is that you lead or are led. Dogs work on a black-

Below: A dog that is taught to be obedient to commands will generally be a happy dog in the home.

and-white system of leadership—if you teach your dog what it can and cannot do and accompany clear, concise commands with the relevant reward, the chances are that your leadership and authority will be respected. Certainly, dogs that are trained well and understand how to follow a series of commands properly are happy dogs. They rarely get into trouble, because they have learned the do's and don'ts of living with people. So the general behavior of dogs is much improved by one critical factor: obedience.

Dogs, without exception, work, train, and become good affectionate companions when the rules are clear. They cannot live beside us in harmony if they try to lead the human pack. So read this book and learn how to lead. By all means, give your dog all the fun, leisure, and outdoor activities you can. Let your children enjoy the companionship and learning curve of dog ownership, but most of all respect your dog for what it is—a magnificent wolf, a versatile and intelligent animal that has left the wild to share the domestic lives of humans like us.

Dog Training—Nine Tips

▶ 1. Before you begin training your dog, be sure you fully understand the exercise and commands you are about to teach. Do not attempt any exercise if you are in doubt.

▶ 2. The motivations for your dog to learn are praise delivered in a pleasant tone of voice, pack behavior, food, and games. Remember this throughout the training program.

▶ 3. Dogs do not understand our language, even though many owners assume they do. You can be sure that if the dog seems to be making errors, the fault lies with the trainer who is not communicating the message clearly enough to the animal. When commanding a dog to do something, make sure that your voice is clear and your tone is firm.

▶ 4. When training, the dog may begin to lose interest. If this is the case, get him to do an exercise he likes and can achieve, praise him for it, and finish training. Play a short game, and try again later in the day.

▶ 5. Never leave a long recall line on your dog when unattended. If the connection ring gets caught on an object, the dog could get hurt. Fixed (nonchoke) collars are best when training.

▶ 6. Be aware that different breeds make progress in training at different rates. It is not important whether your dog learns quickly or slowly, as long as he does learn and changes for the better.

▶ 7. The training lessons should be short. Start with perhaps ten minutes at first and then gradually—if the dog is not losing interest—extend the lessons. Many short lessons are more beneficial than one long one.

▶ 8. Train when your dog is alert. Tired dogs or dogs that have just eaten don't do well.

▶ 9. Avoid making repetitive commands. Dogs are not deaf or stupid. Repeating "Down" ten times does not help. Keeping silent between commands helps the dog to differentiate between the sounds and understand what you want.

► How Dogs Learn

Just like people, dogs learn through association. The dog will want to repeat an action that is "rewarded" with a pleasant consequence, such as a gift of food or a pat, but will be disinclined to repeat actions that meet with unpleasant consequences, such as punishment or a look of disapproval. This is called operant learning. However, unlike us, dogs do not reason; they cannot imagine the consequences of a specific action in the same way that we can—and that's the crux of most problems that dog owners experience. We tend to think that if we show a dog a slipper that he has previously chewed and shout "No," he will make the connection between the chewed slipper and our disapproval—because that is how we would behave.

Well, he's unlikely to make that connection. We may treat a dog like a human, but remember, he can react only like a dog.

Use a firm tone to command.

what behavior is acceptable and what is not. However, don't give up with older dogs; they can unlearn the bad behaviors they've acquired, they just take a little longer and will test you now and again to check whether you've relented and will let them get their own way. The one trait dogs do have in abundance is persistence.

Above and right: Dogs are most responsive to corrective training in the early weeks of their lives.

The Critical Period for Learning

The time when dogs are most sensitive to learning is between five and 12 weeks of age. This is a short-track learning period. I find it important that my puppies should be be imprinted with obedience-training commands and reward techniques during this time. It conditions them to respond to all future advanced training aimed at encouraging positive manners and acceptable behavior. If they are to develop normally, puppies should be socialized with

Above: You need to reprimand a dog or puppy for bad behavior within two seconds of the event so the dog can link your displeasure to its actions.

people and animals and exposed to as many experiences around the home and in the outside world as possible.

Dogs continue to learn throughout their lives, but it is harder to modify the behavior of older dogs with embedded habits. These early weeks are the best time to teach social good manners and obedience and to introduce the dog to

❶

Above right 1, 2, and 3: Beneath a dog's domesticated exterior is an animal whose instincts derive from life in the wild. It is only natural that they should be inquisitive.

Inherited Behavior

Dogs naturally inherit certain drives and behaviors. The degree to which this is true is influenced to an extent by the dog's breed; for example, a Border Collie has strong herding instincts and an acute eye for movement. When a dog like this does not enjoy the usual stimuli or get enough exercise to satisfy its energetic instincts, it may relieve its frustration in another way—perhaps by chasing cyclists or joggers. A ball is often used to redirect such behavior. An anxious or calm temperament can also be inherited, but more often than not this characteristic is exacerbated by the behavior of unwitting owners. Dogs are brimming with wolflike natural drives that have evolved to enable them to survive in the wild, not in your home. So redirecting these innate drives is very important.

Children can help with basic obedience training.

Above right: A dog's behavior is conditioned to a degree by its breed. Dogs with a herding instinct have lots of energy and need lots of exercise.

The search for food is a basic instinct.

❷

❸

23

Inherited behaviors cannot be removed. But they can be altered and lessened or redirected toward less aggravating behavior. However, you will have to accept that terriers will always be highly triggered and prone to bark and hounds liable to follow scents and appear deaf to commands at times. *But do not despair!* In most cases, evidence of a poor temperament, for example a dog that exhibits fears and phobias, is generally due to lack of socialization as a puppy. This sort of behavior can be improved. Some breeds have more robust temperaments than others. Toy breeds can be more hyperactive and fearful, which is probably due to the fact that they are unnaturally small in a world thronging with people with big, clumsy feet.

this action is a rewarding one. Repetition will reinforce this message and produce the desired result. Food, toys, even exercise or time spent with you can all act as powerful reinforcements when teaching a dog new behavior. Rewards when combined with good timing (see below) produce a well-trained dog.

Voice Tone

Words in themselves are meaningless to a dog. If you watch good dog trainers in action, you will notice that they use tone of voice with great flexibility. A word (sound) should be delivered clearly and crisply in short, sharp, one- or two-sylla-

is a potent bonus for a dog, and when used in training, it produces excellent results. If we command our dog to "Sit" and praise him warmly when he sits, the dog will quickly learn that

Above: Try looking at the world from the dog's point of view—puppies have to cope in a world populated by giants.

ble words. In terms of communication, praise and confidence-building words mean a lot to a dog. Don't use long wordy phrases when trying to teach a dog a new lesson; it will simply take longer for the dog to decipher your message.

Reward

To recap, dogs learn by association. Praise—whether in the form of words of encouragement, stroking, or food—

You can use rewards to reinforce good behavior or after a training session.

Above: Time spent playing with your dog helps to build up the bond of friendship between you.

Punishment

Just as a reward is effective in teaching a dog to do something that we approve of, so punishment is effective in discouraging a particular behavior. There are many ways of showing a dog that he is doing something undesirable, such as saying "No" firmly and holding him by the loose skin of the neck or by the collar and looking into his eyes. For example, if a dog playfully nips your hand, then take the dog by the collar, simultaneously command "No," and stare into the dog's eyes for a few seconds. Staring is a statement of dominance, and dogs dislike it. Be careful doing it because it can make some dogs bite from fear or aggression.

Unfortunately, it is human nature to be impatient, and as a result, people use punishment much more often than is necessary to modify canine behavior. It is possible to train a dog while only rarely having recourse to punishment. Rather than hitting a dog when he jumps up, it is much better to teach him to sit and stay and so prevent his being tempted to jump up in the first place. Com-

mand "Sit" when you anticipate the dog is about to jump up. This positive approach is a much better option than falling victim to the negative urge to punish the animal when the action is done. It's worth remembering that dogs did not evolve to fit into a human lifestyle. In fact, it's amazing that they do manage to get along with people so well, considering how little we know about dog communication.

Below 1, 2, 3, and 4: When obedience training a dog, make sure that you use crisp commands and speak them in a clear tone. Words of praise should be offered in a softer tone of voice. Try to keep your verbal commands and any hand signals consistent from day to day.

1

The dog is sitting attentively responsive to the command.

2

The command "Down" is accompanied by a clear movement of the hand and an inclination of the upper body.

3

The dog has responded correctly.

4

Getting Your Timing Right

Timing is critical to all training commands and actions. If you want a dog to learn in a particular situation, the praise or punishment must be given within two seconds following his action. Whether you are offering words of encouragement or discouragement, if you wait too long you may as well not bother. For instance, there is no point in calling your dog in the park, getting irritated when she does not respond immediately, and when she does eventually come back giving her a smack for not returning sooner. The dog will not associate the punishment with something that happened a minute ago; she will simply associate the punishment with coming to you—not the desired result at all. So praise a dog immediately when she obeys your command—she will quickly get the message.

Right: It's all about timing. If you praise a dog for its good behavior or admonish it for poor behavior, do so within two seconds of the event. If you delay longer than this, the dog will not associate your reaction with its action.

Aim for Consistency

It is important that everyone who is involved with correcting your dog's bad habits acts consistently so that the dog does not get confused. If someone is inconsistent in reacting to a bad habit, especially where an undesirable

Below 1 and 2: All the family can take part in obedience training a dog, but it's important that parents should teach children the commands and actions to employ and that all members of the family are consistent when using them.

The command is clear and the hand action unambiguous.

The dog stays as commanded and is alert to its owner.

❶

❷

behavior is embedded in the dog's mind, you will make little progress. You will end up with a dog that sometimes obeys and sometimes doesn't. The psychology is similar to child rearing. Make sure you know exactly what training program you are following, and explain it thoroughly to all family members and any other people concerned. Remember, **for positive results, be consistent.**

Another of our human failings is our reluctance to be critical of ourselves. Nearly all owners who consult me about their dogs' behavioral problems repeat the same mantra, "He won't listen, I've told him ten times, he just won't learn." I often film them trying to instruct their dog and then play the tape back to them. This is what they hear, "Oscar sit, sit down, sit here, stop it, just **sit** Oscar, Oscar **sit down**, you bad dog," and on it goes. Now what use is that? The command is "Sit." How the dog is supposed to realize that one word in all that ramble should lead him to a sitting position defeats me...and the dog. People usually get the message after watching the tape. It can be quite amusing and we can laugh about our human foibles. Remember that we are conditioned to teaching other humans who can solve problems with their big brains and complex reasoning abilities. Dogs just do not work that way.

Below 1: Dogs are quite prepared to defer to and obey other members of the family pack, even relatively young children. Note how this Dalmatian is standing, looking alertly at the girl, much in the same way as the dog focuses on the mother in the picture on the opposite page.

Below 2: The girl's body language is distinct and her voice commands short and crisp, as her mother has taught her. The result is that the dog is sitting obediently and waiting for further commands. Consistency reaps dividends.

Guilty or Not?

Many people describe their dog as looking guilty when he has urinated on the carpet or chewed the leg of a chair. They infer from this that their dog knows that he has done wrong. In most cases, the dog looks guilty not because it feels any remorse, but because it has learned to read your body language or tone of voice and it associates these with your anger and subsequent punishments. Dogs do not feel guilt as we do. Only when you accept this fact can retraining begin. Showing signs of being frightened is not evidence of a guilty conscience; it's straightforward fear.

Don't expect your dog to value material possessions. He can't tell the difference between designer clothes and a pair of old, worn-out jeans. To a dog there's no such thing as your food and his food, it's all just food—until he is taught otherwise. Dogs need to be taught step-by-step if they are to end up as good, sociable companions. And when you are trying to correct a dog that has done something wrong, if possible do try to praise a positive behavior rather than just punishing the behavior you don't want. It makes life easier for all concerned.

Below 1, 2, and 3: If you spot your dog doing this, you will almost inevitably interpret its expression in picture 3 as a guilty look. But the dog is not feeling guilty—she is more likely apprehensive because she knows your body language and expects punishment.

Ignore—A Powerful Dominance Statement

If your dog tries to dominate your life by excessive attention seeking using domination techniques like barking, jumping up, nudging, pawing, whining, etc., then introduce the Ignore response to your dog. In my view, this is one of the most effective training methods that we can use. Put simply, you ignore the behavior that you wish to stop or reduce and conversely give attention to behavior you wish to encourage. That's the easy bit, the hard bit is ignoring very calculating, clever dogs that display inordinate persistence in getting their own way. These dogs are often skilled in manipulation. If you persevere and are consistent, you will

find that few dogs go on repeating a behavior that is unrewarding. Puppies or less practiced dogs are, of course, much more responsive to the Ignore method of training.

To give an example—suppose your dog keeps pestering you. You say, "Get

Left: It is difficult to harden your heart and not respond to the pleading looks, but the Ignore response is a very powerful, way of discouraging behavior that you want to deter.

off—stop it," perhaps you push the dog down physically or give the dog eye contact. Many dogs see these actions as rewarding, even if they are accompanied by an aggressive tone of voice. The art of Ignore psychology is to remain aloof; imagine your dog isn't there, even though he's driving you mad. After a week or so of being unable to gain your attention, the annoying behaviors begin naturally to fade. I have yet to find a dog that did not alter significantly when the owner employed the Ignore training correctly and consistently.

Below: When dealing with dominant dogs, it is often helpful to restrict their movements by using a wall-mounted hook to which their leads can be secured.

Ignore—Recap

When your dog is pestering you or attempting to get your attention, remember the following:

- **Don't give him eye contact.**
- **Try not to shove or push the dog away physically—he may interpret this as play.**
- **Don't shout at the dog.**
- **Use the hook restriction program for a dominant dog when necessary (see pages 48–51).**
- **Implement the dominance reduction program (see pages 44–47), which will markedly improve behavior.**

How Dogs Learn—Recap

- **• The critical period for the formation of a dog's temperament is when a puppy is between five and 12 weeks of age.**
- **• Different breeds inherit different behavioral tendencies, just as they inherit different physical tendencies.**
- **• Tone of voice and the ability to use your voice effectively in training are vital.**
- **• Rewards should be given within two seconds following a desired action.**
- **• Reprimands should be given within two seconds following an undesired action.**
- **• Timing and consistency are vital so that a link between the trainer's commands and the desired action is consistently forged.**
- **• Guilt is a human concept, not a canine one.**
- **• Ignore is a powerful learning tool that dogs understand.**

Training Equipment

Basic Dog Training

When dogs need training, the first essential is a collar and lead. Most dogs respond well to training, and the results are generally good. A dog, like a child, needs an education to prepare it for life in our world. If he does not learn what he can—and cannot—do, he will eventually do just what he wants to, acting purely on instinct. Conflict with his owner is almost inevitable.

For example, it is instinctive for a dog to eat any food available, not only in the dog bowl but even off the dining room table. To a dog it is simply natural behavior, until taught otherwise. In fact, a human baby will do exactly the same until she is taught not to, and yet while most people view the baby's action as innocent, the dog is labeled a thief and bad. That perception or expectation of the animal is unfair to the dog and it highlights how human perceptions and expectations of dog behavior need adjusting.

The lead is looped to shorten it so that the dog stays close to the walker.

Below: A well-fitting and sturdy collar is a must for any dog that is going to share your home. It enables you to take a firm hold of the dog should the need arise, and by attaching a lead to the collar, you can keep the dog securely under your control.

Above: One of the basic disciplines that you must teach a dog is to walk to heel on a lead. Once the dog has learned to obey, even children can safely walk the animal.

Breaking Bad Habits

Many companies produce excellent and innovative equipment to help assist the dog owner in reeducating the dog and correcting its behavior. This section explains what is readily available and how it should be used. Unfortunately, equipment is all too often employed as a quick fix, but without some instruction in training methods, quick-fix solutions are usually doomed to failure. However, when the equipment is used by people with experience and knowledge of canine behavior or with the assistance and guidance of a qualified dog trainer or canine behavioral practitioner, it can help speed up retraining and help to ameliorate even very severe cases of bad behavior.

Most equipment is suitable for use both with sensitive dogs and puppies (SDP) and with determined and dominant dogs (DD), but some is only to be used on DD dogs. When reading the descriptions in this chapter, assume that the equipment described can be used on both SDP and DD unless otherwise stated.

Retractable Leads

Leads that extend and rewind have many uses in helping to reform a dog's behavior. I use one when introducing a family dog to a new pet, whether a cat or dog. It allows retractable distance on the lead, which enables the dog to move as near to the new pet as you wish without your immediate presence imposing on the dog. Dog-to-dog aggression is another area where such a lead is useful. Many dogs react aggressively to other dogs when attached to a lead. However, when the handler pays out the retractable lead, the absence of the expected restriction takes the edge off the antagonist. The handler is not nearby to "support" the aggressor, so the dog has to stand alone. This flexibility often reduces tension and thereby aggression.

Long Lines

Use nylon line (between 20 and 50 feet/6–15 m long) that can be purchased from a hardware or a boating shop. Place a dog hook at one end to attach to a collar and form a loop for a handle at the

other (always wear gloves when using the line). This is very effective when used in recall training with a young dog.

> ### Guidance on Leads and Collars
>
> ▷ **Dog leads: Leather leads are the best. Ideally, they should measure about four to six feet (1.2–2 m) in length.**
>
> ▷ **Dog collars: Again leather is to be preferred but nylon collars are also useful.**
>
> ▷ **Martingale collars: These are safe to use as a martingale collar does not tighten fully on a dog's neck.**
>
> ▷ **Check chains and slip (choke) collars: These tighten on a dog's neck as the dog pulls. They should be used only in specific circumstances and with a qualified trainer—they are not for general use and should never be used on puppies or small breeds.**

Retractable leads tend to stay tight.

Above and right: The retractable lead unwinds from a spool in the container against the pressure of a spring. By pressing a button near the handle, the line can be locked at any length.

Left: A retractable lead is useful when you want to introduce a dog to another pet in the household. The fact that the line unreels from the holder allows the dog some freedom to move forward and make the acquaintance of the other animal, but you can retract it if he shows signs of aggression.

Dog-Walking Harnesses

These are harnesses specially designed and fitted to the dog's body. They work by making it uncomfortable for the dog to pull the owner when on a walk, and conversely they are comfortable to wear when the dog stops pulling.

Car Harnesses

These allow you to secure your dog in the back of the car by attaching the harness to a seat belt. They are useful when a dog's movements in the car need to be controlled and can be helpful when dealing with dogs that suffer from car sickness (see Chapter 18).

As this picture (left) shows, dogs can still open their mouths to pant in a head halter.

Above: A dog-walking harness discourages a dog from pulling by exerting pressure under its "armpits."

Head Halters

(for determined and dominant dogs only) Like the harness, this is used to stop dogs pulling, but in this case, it fits over the dog's muzzle. It allows the dog's mouth to open as usual so that he can breathe normally. When the dog pulls ahead of his owner, the face collar checks the dog's head back toward the owner, making it uncomfortable or awkward for the dog to pull. They are particularly good for large dogs or when the owner is not particularly mobile or able to control powerful dogs that pull. They also have a calming effect on some aggressive dogs. You first need to learn to use one correctly for it to be effective and safe.

The Muzzle *(for determined and dominant or aggressive dogs only)*

Useful for all problems of aggression or dogs that scavenge food. When first using a muzzle, it is most important to introduce it slowly so that the dog does not associate it with a bad experience. Most people rush the introduction and then get worried by the dog's stressed reaction to it. Here's how you should do it. The method also applies to head halters.

First get the dog to sit while wearing a lead and collar. Have several juicy tid-

Left: This retriever is perfectly comfortable while walking calmly by his owner. But if he were to surge ahead, the face collar would cause his head to be pulled up.

Left: If you accustom a dog to wearing a muzzle by using tidbits to reward good behavior, she should get used to it reasonably quickly. Travel to the park by car also rewards the dog for wearing a muzzle with the prospect of a walk together.

Above: A cage-type muzzle has a mesh of slats through which you can give a dog tidbits and food rewards.

Most of the food rewards suggested in this book will need to be stuffed inside a rubber toy for the dog to lick out. Therefore, dry food won't usually work well. Instead, aim for food that is sticky, such as most meat-based diets.

The Food Toy

Rubber toys in which food can be concealed are used to help cope with boredom, destructive behavior, and aggression and for teaching dogs to be alone for short periods in the yard or other rooms in the house. Dogs are kept occupied as they work at the toy to get at the food contained in it. It is also useful for puppy training, for crate training, and as a way of stimulating all dogs mentally.

bits at hand. Put the muzzle on the dog (he must be able to open his mouth with a muzzle fitted), and then reward the dog with a tidbit fed through the muzzle. Leave it on the dog for a few minutes, remove it, then give another food reward. The dog should now associate wearing the muzzle with a reward.

This needs to be repeated three times daily for about ten minutes a time **for three days**. On day 4, attach the lead and fit the muzzle to the dog as usual, then walk the dog a short way in the house or yard, and reward the dog at frequent intervals. If the dog panics or attempts to rub his head on the floor (which is normal), distract him with the food and use your lead to make him sit.

It's also useful to leave the muzzle on the dog in the house twice daily for about ten to 15 minutes. When the dog begins to accept the muzzle without fuss, then you are beginning to reach normalization. Most dogs resent the muzzle at first

but quickly adapt and associate it with food rewards and walks. Once you can walk the dog around the house or yard without adverse reaction, you are ready for normal outdoor use.

Natural Diet Food and Food Rewards

Though food is not the only aid used in training, it can be a very potent influence. Food is vital for body maintenance and significantly affects behavior in dogs. Dogs, like people, should be given a high-quality, balanced diet, preferably one free of chemicals, colorants, and other additives. Some people believe such additives can adversely affect behavior and find that feeding a home-prepared diet including fresh meat and other ingredients improves their dogs' behavior, especially aggression and anxiety-related behaviors. Such a diet should follow recipes and precautions developed by canine nutritionists.

Below: The food toy is very useful in diverting a dog from a bad behavior by giving her a pleasurable distraction on which to concentrate instead.

Deterrent Sprays

These products are harmless, unpleasant-tasting liquid sprays, and they are very useful in the early stages of teaching puppies not to chew valuable household furnishings and items.

I have recently used one to stop Saphie, a puppy Cairn, from chewing. Puppies are naturally inquisitive, and Saphie, like all puppies, explores her world with her teeth and nose. Under my desk there is a jungle of computer wires and cables. I can't see what she is doing all the time, so I spray the cables with the bitter spray every day. First experiences are critical in dog training, and once she has had a taste of that spray, the electric cables are off the menu.

Above: The remote training scent collar can be activated at long range by the use of small handheld control device.

Above: Deterrent sprays use bitter-tasting, but otherwise harmless, liquids to discourage a dog from unwanted behaviors. This application should stop the dog play biting the young girl's arm.

Remote Training Collar

(for determined and dominant dogs only)
This is a scent collar that works by remote control at short distances and that emits a jet of pungent-smelling, but harmless, citronella spray. I have used this to help teach recall to dogs that ignore other training methods in order to get them back on command.

Stopping dogs scavenging food or eating animal and bird feces, which could ultimately make them very ill, can also be helped with the collar. To use the collar effectively, you do need to understand how dogs learn. Timing is essential, and you should get help from a dog trainer to learn how to put the device into correct operation. It is not intended as a way for you to relieve your frustration and punish the animal—it should never be used in that manner. Though the spray is innocuous, like all training devices, it can still spook a few dogs when inappropriately used.

Training Disks

These devices have two distinct applications when used effectively. When they are thrown near a misbehaving dog, the disks interrupt the action the dog is pursuing and produce an unpleasant association. Preconditioning the dog to react to the sound of the disks is the second way of using the disks. You can use a bunch of keys to obtain a similar effect, but the disks are far more practical in application and will work on most, though not all, dogs. Be careful when using them with puppies, however.

The disks work in the following way:
- The dog learns a sound (the clatter of the disks) and associates it with whatever it is doing wrong.
- It associates the sound with a command, "No."
- Eventually the dog responds instantly to the command "No" without the disks being used.

Most dogs learn to stop an undesirable behavior when the disks are used. Eventually we can wean most dogs off the sound of the disks, but occasionally very persistent dogs will need a reminder of the disks being thrown.

Above: By using the disks, you can teach a dog that it can take the tidbit only when you command "Eat." If the dog lunges at the food unprompted, the disks are thrown noisily on the floor near the dog's food.

How to Use the Disks

Most dogs like food so, using a collar and lead for control, take a tasty tidbit between two fingers and with the dog nearby pretend to place the food on a low table. When the dog goes to grab the food, shut your hand tight, preventing the food from being taken, and **simultaneously** throw the disks down near your hand while commanding "No." If you are dealing with a really greedy dog that catches your fingers with his teeth, get somebody else to control the dog on a collar and lead for added safety

The dog will be startled and will back away, which is what we want. Some dogs need half a dozen throws of the disks and the associated jangle before they get the idea that the food is not to be eaten from the table. The idea is that the dog learns that when he decides to grab the food from the table, the disks will clatter on the floor. If the dog then eats the food from his bowl, a calmly whispered "Good dog" can reinforce the message.

Now let's use that learned behavior to cope with other problems like jumping up, barking, or pestering. Once the dog has got the message that "No" means "No" in association with the sound of the disks being thrown or rattled in your hand, you can transpose the training technique. For example, if your dog is pestering you for attention, command "No" and simultaneously throw the disks down near the dog's feet. This should stop the unwanted action. When order is restored, a calm "Good dog" can be said.

Dog Stop Alarms

(for determined and dominant dogs only)
These aerosol-type alarms work by emitting a sharp, high-pitched noise when activated by the owner. They startle the dog long enough for you to interrupt what he is doing and issue a countercommand or offer a reward for another action. For example, if the dog begins to show aggression toward another dog, you activate the alarm—the behavior is interrupted—you then heel off with the dog either using voice commands or some toy or tidbit as a distraction.

Step 1: The disks are very effective at stopping a dog from pestering for attention.

Step 2: By commanding "No" while throwing the disks on the ground, the dog comes to associate the sound of the disks with the order "No."

Step 3: After a while, the dog should respond just to the command "No" without the need for the disks to be thrown as a reinforcement.

❶

❷

❸

Below: It pays to condition and train a dog to spend time on her own on her bed. The dog will feel secure there, and you can use the command "Bed" when you want to be left alone.

Dog Doors

These are like large cat flaps and are generally used when housebreaking dogs or to allow dogs access to the yard when you are out.

Indoor Cages and Playpens

These are useful for housebreaking a puppy or controlling a destructive dog.

Water Pistols

Water pistols (or even clean dish-washing liquid bottles) can be used to squirt water at a misbehaving dog. They work rather like the dog stop alarm by giving the dog a short, sharp surprise and are especially useful when puppies begin to nibble any kind of forbidden item in the home.

Dog Beds

When a puppy is newly brought into the home, it feels very insecure and a little lost. Adaptable as dogs are, one can help the process of acclimatization by teaching the dog that he has a place where he can lie without being in the way of pedestrian traffic around the home. I usually put a small bed in a cage or puppy pen when a puppy first arrives. The puppy finds the texture and warmth reassuring and, as he is kept in the pen for short periods and at night, he is naturally conditioned to sleep in the soft, warm bed. As the weeks pass and the puppy's feelings of security and well-being increase, I begin to move the bed around the kitchen area. As the puppy is now conditioned to sleep or rest in the bed, he will seek it out for sleep and relaxation.

As time goes by, I add another link to the training routine by giving the com-

Above and right: Playing with rope toys such as this helps to keep a dog physically fit and mentally stimulated. What's more, playtime is fun for you too!

mand "Bed" and pointing to it. I train the dog to go to the bed and lie down, and I reward him with a treat. This command is useful when visitors arrive who do not necessarily want dogs near them or when you are occupied around the house and don't want the dog to interfere. You can put the bed in any part of the house, or in the car for travel, and the dog will still relax in it as the early conditioning has done its job.

Dogs love playing with tug-of-war-type toys like this. Take care with dominant dogs, however; they may view the game as a contest they must win.

Car Ramps

Teaching dogs how to get in and out of cars is a major task if the dog is large and the owner infirm or not very strong. Ramps help to teach dogs what you require and allow them to get into a car until they are old enough to jump in and out of their own accord. Because many new cars sit high off the road, small dogs and puppies can also learn to enter and exit a car with a ramp.

Carrier Cages and Crates

Carrier cages/crates and dog guards are useful in a car from a safety point of view and can help prevent unwanted behavior like jumping about on the car seats.

Dog harnesses are also useful, especially if you drive a sedan rather that an SUV or station wagon. They are made in a variety of sizes and clip on to the rear seat belts. They are comfortable for dogs to wear and prevent them from jumping about. They also help stop dogs from becoming overexcited because they are restrained.

Toys, Balls

These are essential for all sorts of mind-stimulating games to assist the dog's mental development and are also used in the programs that deal with separation anxiety and recall training.

Above: Nowadays toys for dogs come in a wonderful array of shapes, sizes, and squeaks. Playing with your pet helps to form a strong family bond.

Whistle

As essential adjunct to recall training; the use of a whistle for this purpose is described fully in Chapter 4.

Above: An indoor cage or pen is invaluable when you are trying to toilet train a young puppy. It is also sensible to teach a puppy from an early age that it is normal to spend time on its own away from you.

The Dominant Dog

Dominant, boisterous, pushy, in the way, always tripping you up, in your face—these are words that people use to describe the dominant dog. In fact, these dogs are like children who have not been taught consistent discipline from a young age. Neither of them understands our values of right and wrong. However, there the similarity ends because you can explain to a child what you want, but dogs live only for the moment and explanations are just a waste of breath. In a way dominant dogs live in a world where normal signals of communication between owner and dog have become blurred. This would not be the case in the wild—for a wolf pack to run smoothly there must be few misunderstandings between pack members. But dogs aren't wolves, so they may need guidance.

Above: Pawing, nudging, and butting in when you are busy are other ways in which a dog tries to assert its dominance.

Left: A textbook case of a dominant dog pulling on the lead quite oblivious to its owner's commands.

Below: Airedales are strong and energetic dogs. On occasions their assertiveness can make them hard to handle.

Problem Signs

Dominant dogs can exhibit some or all of the behaviors mentioned above. In addition, these dogs will often dive through doorways before you or be the first to get into or out of the car without waiting for your cue. They are often more inclined to pull on the lead and to drag you around the park from one dog to the next or from one sniff to another. Significantly, when doing this, the dog never turns his head to view his "pack leader's" reactions because he does not feel the need to do so, even though you are tugging on the lead and shouting all sorts of commands at him. Such ineffectual owners are nothing more than background noise to a dominant dog.

Top dog! You could not ask for a more graphic illustration of how a dog can sometimes seek to dominate its owner.

Owners describe how they use various ploys to divert the dog or fool its skills of anticipation so as not to be dragged hither and thither. Do any of these complaints sound familiar, "I never pick my car keys up first," "I can't get the dog's lead on the collar because he gets so excited," "I have to put the dog in the car before my children because otherwise he will knock them over," "I can't eat dinner in peace because he

▶ Tactics to Elicit Attention

- ▶ Adopting a doleful sad look
- ▶ Barking
- ▶ Fetching a toy
- ▶ Grabbing something that is off-limits
- ▶ Nudging your hand for strokes
- ▶ Pawing
- ▶ Pressing their body against you or leaning on you
- ▶ Rolling over for pats and tickles
- ▶ Shivering and shaking
- ▶ Sitting on your foot
- ▶ Whining

barks," "I can't get the cat's food ready without locking him in another room." What is constant here is the "I can't" refrain. The dominant dog rules supreme—aren't dogs clever!

Above 1, 2, and 3: How often is this little scene played out? Your dog runs to fetch a toy, comes hurtling back, and drops it at your feet expecting you to play. Dominant dogs try to set the domestic agenda; instead you must assert your control.

Causes of Dominance

Dominant dogs have a strong innate drive to be the leader. Although the strength of this varies from dog to dog and breed to breed, dominance is very much compounded by how they have learned, through endless practice, to get your attention and so their own way.

There is no equality in dog society; you either lead or you are led. This does not mean that we humans cannot develop a trusting and enjoyable relationship with our pet dogs. On the contrary, a dog that knows its position in

the hierarchy of the family pack is undoubtedly a happy and contented dog. Moreover, it is a less anxious dog.

The following programs are quick ways of psychologically teaching your dog how to behave in the way that you want. You must show by your example and your behavior, as well as by lack of response to her demanding overtures, that you are the leader. Remember, you are trying to accustom a dog that did not evolve to live in a human household to coexist with humans who don't speak "wolf language."

Altering Behavior

To change the way a dog behaves, we have to keep rewards very clearly defined and offer them only for the behavior that you wish to teach or encourage. Unpleasant behavior, like jumping up on you or pestering endlessly for attention, **can** be stopped without confrontation. The dog is obviously not aware that you have chores to fulfill. Like a young child, she has no concept of time or responsibility, only what she wants to happen at that moment.

You will need some additional equipment and training procedures to bring the embedded, unpleasant behavior under control when dealing with very strong-willed dogs or dogs that have been badly behaved for a long time and know most of the tricks of their manipulative trade. Though dog-training equipment—such as training disks—will

Right: It's obvious that he thinks that he's the top dog in the household. But that attitude can be changed.

Below 1, 2, and 3: Defining dominance is very difficult at times. What one owner considers bad behavior, such as jumping up and demanding attention like this, may not be a problem at all for another owner.

Getting your attention on demand means that the dog is getting her own way, just what the dominant dog wants.

❶

❷

1

2

3

Left and below 1, 2, and 3:
As the section on training disks in Chapter 2 explained, timing is critical. Throwing the training disks after the dog is already sitting is too late for teaching her not to jump up.

3

help achieve a quick result in the short term, for the long term the same dog will have to learn how to behave well. You can only do this by treating her like a dog and not as a little human. This means altering her behavior by patient, long-term, nonconfrontational training methods. Obstinate bad behavior has to be remolded. However, dogs are malleable creatures and, when given clear crisp directions backed up with suitable rewards, are able to change.

If you read carefully the section on how dogs learn (pages 22–29) and understand that the dog's learning association time is about two seconds, you will know that you must link an action to a reward or unpleasant experience within that time frame. I deliberately avoid the word "punishment" here because, in my view, it is the wrong word

to describe what you are doing to the dog. However, the word does seem to fit into the human concept of retribution and I occasionally use it for fluidity in the narrative, but do try to remember that a dog does not view punishment, nor understand the meaning of the word, as we do. The human concept of punishment means nothing to a dog. It simply learns that an action is followed by an enjoyable experience or it is not. If an action ceases to be enjoyable or if it goes unrewarded, the dog will eventually cease to act in this way.

41

Jumping Up for Attention

A common example of unacceptable behavior is exhibited by the dominant dog that is big, pushy, and jumps up on you. This can hurt, and the behavior has to be stopped. Dogs instinctively want to be near your mouth, just like their wild counterparts where jumping up can lead to food rewards in the shape of regurgitated morsels of food from a senior pack member. Another reason most dogs jump up is because as puppies they were offered touch, voice, and/or food rewards when they cutely placed their little puppy paws on your lap when you were seated. In time the behavior becomes more prolific due to more rewards (unwittingly proffered) and, as the dog gets bigger, so does the problem.

As an adult dog, the game is now fixed in its psyche. Often humans will employ a strategy of avoidance to minimize the annoyance of the dog jumping up. This in turn often makes the dog more ingenious at **getting attention** through jumping up. Game, set, and match to the dog!

As the dog gets bigger, more agile, and faster, the action becomes more unpleasant and people begin to push the dog off after an initial gentle pat (reward) or a stroke thinking, "That's enough, he'll be satisfied with that." The dominant dog reads this as a powerful reinforcement reward—the pat does not signify "Now go away" but is interpreted as a pat for being persistent. By forcing its attention onto visitors or family members, it demonstrates its right to be dominant.

Some people are more strict or less disposed to indulge the dog, and often you will see a dog make choices about whom to pester in order to get the most attention. This beautifully demonstrates their ability to learn how to get a reward and to anticipate from whom the best rewards will come. They learn quickly, but if you know how to teach a dog what you want it to learn, you can turn this aptitude to your advantage to retrain dominant dogs.

Above: The bigger the dog, the bigger the problem can be when he insists on getting on your lap.

The Human Factor

Certain types of dog owner are more likely to be dominated by their dogs than others, and they are often on the receiving end of aggressive displays. It is not unusual for people who are not particularly assertive, or who have weak personalities, to spoil their dogs endlessly, treating them like children. They avoid facing up to an annoying

Below: It's hard to resist a puppy when he puts his little paws against your leg looking for a pat. But by continually indulging the puppy, we may imprint a behavior pattern that seems less acceptable later in the dog's life when he still climbs up for attention. Praise should be given only when the puppy or adult dog is on four, not two, legs.

behavior preferring to live in hope that it will mend itself. Of course, these people are most at risk, but a strong-willed animal may try to assert its dominance over any owner, however masterful that person may be.

Certain breeds of dog seem to have an innate propensity to dominance, including the so-called guard breeds, like Rottweilers, Dobermans, and Mastiffs. But other breeds, too, like Cocker and English and Welsh Springer Spaniels plus many of the terriers, can display this temperament. Small breeds like the Shih Tzu may look like lovable bundles of fluff, but despite their size, they are frequently dominant and aggressive by nature. The giant breeds like Maremma Sheepdogs, Great Pyrenese, and Bernese Mountain Dogs can also exhibit their fair share of aggression. However, I have seen dominance aggression in all breeds, so none is really exempt from this characteristic.

Right: *This picture graphically illustrates the problem when large dogs try to assert dominance through jumping up. The person is leaning back, showing amusement mixed with some discomfort at being on the receiving end of this display.*

On its hind legs, the Dalmatian stands nearly as tall as the woman.

Coping with Dominance— First Achieve Psychological Demotion

The following suggestions are not to be viewed as punishments or means of retribution. They are ways of starting a new regime in which you are established as the leader and your dog accepts you as such. He will learn how to behave and become well mannered and good-tempered. This program is only for dogs that have behavior problems stemming from overblown self-images and a desire to dominate.

It is sensible that the following program should be introduced over a period of one or two weeks.

Below 1: Dominant dogs like to take possession of, or occupy, significant parts of the house, such as the living room sofa or your nice comfortable bed.

• If your dog sleeps in your bedroom, ban it from there immediately. This includes the stairway. Use a baby gate(s) to restrict access if necessary.

• When walking about the house, make your dog get out of your way. Do not walk around it. Use your foot to nudge the dog gently out of the way. If your dog is aggressive or may bite, do not use this method. Instead, push a wheeled shopping bag or a push broom ahead of you to clear a pathway.

• Give no tidbits or treats (except for reward or training purposes).

• Remove all toys, balls, chews, and similar articles. Only use them when you choose to do so.

Left: Don't allow the dog to barge ahead and push through a door before you. Shut the door firmly in his face to deny him the privilege of going first. Continue to do this until he lets you take precedence.

Right: He'll get his food only after you have finished eating.

Below 2: *You must take charge, command the dog to get off the bed, and ban the dog from the room totally.*

2

Below 3: *Keep the door shut and, if necessary, use a baby gate to keep upstairs totally off limits.*

3

- Stop petting your dog for no reason, and I mean totally. All petting is now **earned**.
- If there are certain rooms, seats, or areas that the dog habitually occupies, then ban him from them. Use a baby gate to prevent access to stairways or rooms if necessary.
- Don't let your dog go through a doorway before you. If you open a door and he tries to push ahead of you, slam the door in his face (make sure that the door does not hit him). You may have to do this many times to get him to learn to wait and defer to you. The dog learns that when you call him through a doorway it is

Left: *Pack up the toys and put them somewhere out of the dog's reach. Playing with toys will now be something that you, not the dog, will initiate.*

safe. When he pushes ahead of you, the door slams shut.

- When preparing your dog's food or your own meals, make sure that your dog is aware that he will be given his food only after you have completed your meal.

- When watching television or reading a book, don't unwittingly stroke your dog when nudged. **Ignore him**. Leaders ignore the solicitations of lower-ranking pack members unless it suits them—that is what keeps them as leaders.
- If you live in a standard size house, only allow your dog into the den by invitation between three and six times daily for periods of between half an hour and one hour. Then tell him to leave, and use a lead and collar if necessary to make sure the dog obeys your command "Out."
- If you are using the hook restriction program (see below), try having several hooks positioned in different rooms to help you when first teaching the dog to stay out of your room.

  You may wonder what is the point of having a dog if you cannot touch or

Left 1: When obedience training is correctly done, even small children can control big dogs. But it is important that all family members use the same commands.

❶

Above: This is the situation that you are trying to rectify. The dog has become habituated to getting her own way—the unfortunate owner is on the floor.

Right: This is more like it. The person has possession of the chair and is reading in peace without persistent nudging and interruption from the dog. It may take months to get to this stage, but persistence should pay off.

praise him. Well, you have to make a choice: either you put up with the problem and watch it become worse or you become tough and do something about it so that you can both enjoy a happier relationship later on.

How long should the above methods be pursued? Well, that depends on many factors, including how badly behaved or dominating your dog is and how long the problem has been in evidence. I find that after about three months, one can ease up on some of

Below 2: The firm command "Sit," backed up by a hand gesture, produces the desired result.

How to Take Charge— Obedience Training

Obedience training to dogs is what schooling is to children, a way of educating the child or, in this case, the dog, to fit into our complex society. Dogs

Below 3: Here the dog is responding to the command "Down" and again the child motions to show the dog what to do. The mother keeps hold of the collar and lead during the exercise to ensure that the dog is under control at all times.

that understand the basic commands of "Sit," "Stand," "Down," "Stay," "Come," plus "No" and "Good boy/ girl" have a communication language that benefits both parties. Like children they need time to learn, and repetition is a great teacher. The more consistent you are with your commands, the easier it is for a dog to learn. Dogs can be confused when they are expected to act in response to an alternative word for the same command if they have not learned it.

Having trained your dog to obey certain commands, you can then use this control to influence his behavior. For example, if he will not move off the couch, we can command "Come," then "Down," and then "Stay." Your dog will understand the new ideas and, with the prompting of tone of voice rewards and maybe the odd tidbit, he will learn to obey and accept you as leader. This will take time. However, it **does work if you are consistent** and patient and make the necessary long-term effort. Now many experienced readers may say, "I've tried all that but he's still difficult." Read on because I have some new methods to help you control your dog.

2

3

the ignoring and the absence of stroking procedures, but many dogs have to be kept on the new regimen for life otherwise they return to their old ways. You have to judge your own circumstances and gauge the results.

Right 4: Lesson over—now it's time for grooming and perhaps a game. Once the dog accepts that it must obey commands, the balance of the family pack is back on an even keel.

4

Phase Two—
The Hook Restriction Program

The next step is to implement structured training routines that will prevent your dog from performing ingrained bad habits. You will now make the decisions about what happens around you and when and how your dog will behave. I call this reforming the dog's familiarity of its home geography—i.e., your house and yard.

People Arriving
at Your Home

A big dog out of control is a daunting prospect.

This section describes how to change and calm your dog's behavior in the home. I concentrate on the house because that is where most people seem least able to control a dominant dog. It is the center of your joint worlds—a busy meeting place, particularly if children are about. After the following training regimen has been put into practice, clients normally tell me how quiet and well behaved their dog has become. "He's a different dog." It's so simple to accomplish—here's how.

Right: A dog that persistently does this to a visitor will quickly start to lose you friends unless you do something about it.

Below 1, 2, and 3: By using a food-filled toy in association with the hook restriction method, a dog comes to associate being tethered with a pleasant reward.

❶

❸

The Kong is a rubber toy that is used for play. We use it in many dog behavior programs. However, you can safely adapt several toys that are strong, are nonedible, and have a central cavity that makes extracting sticky meat foods a slow affair for your dog, keeping her mind occupied as she works out the food.

Dogs that show dominance and leap boisterously all over visitors can be made to learn that the arrival of visitors will be rewarded with a pleasant experience that has nothing to do with jumping up. We are aiming to redirect their energy to this new toy and the associated links of a hook and lead, as explained below. The toy is attractive because it is stuffed with your dog's daily diet, and that means all of the diet, not just tidbits. Hide the dog's food dish away for a few months. Of course, a bowl of water should still be available.

How the Dog Sees the Situation

To retrain a dominant dog, it is important to understand who is leading and who is led. Most dominant dogs have learned a set of "triggers" to which they respond. The owner then reacts to the dog and is, in consequence, led. For example, a guest arrives at the door. That is the dog's trigger, and he begins to become very excited. Usually he will also have learned how to avoid being caught and controlled, and so when the guest enters your home, it's a free-for-all. As you and your guests walk to the lounge, the dog will be demanding to be petted, jumping up, barking, and performing other disruptive behaviors.

You may try your best to control the dog's actions, but experience has taught her how to persist and wear down most people's resistance. When a dog forces

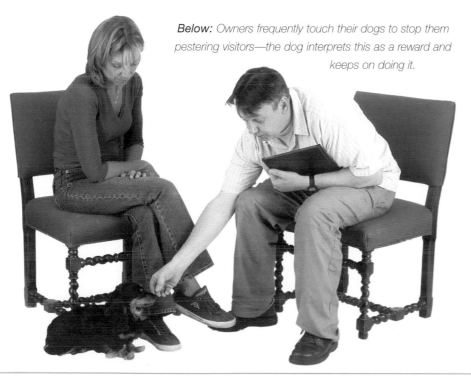

Left: If a visitor takes notice of a dog that is demanding attention, the dog has won a small victory and is liable to repeat the behavior.

herself on people, they generally start to pet her, believing that by making this concession the dog will be satisfied. Once acknowledged, they think she will stop. Most owners also "pet touch" their own dog when trying to calm her down or stop her misbehaving. The dog learns that her actions produce this flurry of touch, eye contact, and voice acknowledgment. Success is the dog's reward, and so the disruptive behavior is embedded. There is no motivation to stop, so she does not stop and the dog is prepared to put up with the occasional display of anger from her owner. **The dog has learned the following scenario:**

The doorbell/knocker sounds. I (the dog) must act quickly and become excited because there are two powerful rewards.

1 The visitor is forced to stroke/pet/stop and pay attention to me as a demanding dog.

2 My owner gives me petting (just holding the dog qualifies as a reward), shouts at me, and generally gets equally excited by the arrival.

The chaos that ensues is often unwittingly made worse by the actions of the owner until the dog becomes a complete nuisance.

Below: Owners frequently touch their dogs to stop them pestering visitors—the dog interprets this as a reward and keeps on doing it.

How to Take Full Control

The first remedial action is to halt your dog's well-tried disruptive routine in its tracks. **You** must decide what will happen in the house and when. Patience for the first five days is critical. No anger, no shouting, no manhandling of the dog. Dogs are basically opportunists and will seek every opportunity to practice their wiles. This new routine is also manipulative, making use of the fact that dogs love their leads and associate them with being walked, so getting the dog on a lead should not be too difficult.

Equipment Required

In the short term, use of the training disks or a water pistol (see pages 34–37) will probably stop, or at least interrupt, your dog's shenanigans. The dog will now associate jumping up with the unpleasant sound of the disks clattering on the floor, providing they are used consistently when the dog jumps up.

You will also need a lead—four to six feet (1.2–2 m) long—and two or more hooks attached to a baseboard, wall, or other solid fixing point around your home. A food toy filled with tasty, sticky food is also required. If one hook is set into a baseboard about 4 inches (10 cm) from the floor, you can easily drop the end loop of the lead over it. Don't fix the hooks in a walk-through area. Remember to ensure that any baseboard used is firmly fixed, as a large dog could pull a loose one away from the wall.

Below 1 and 2: Getting your dog accustomed to spending time on its own attached to the hook helps to break the pattern of disruptive behavior.

1

2

3

Left: If your dog remains quiet on the hook while visitors are present, you can eventually reward him with a quiet word of praise and release him from the tether.

Praise and touch rewards happen only when you say so.

While you are at home, place your dog on the hook, using a lead and collar, for about 20 minutes at a time three times a day. Condition the dog so that you release him only when he is quiet and relaxed. If he becomes overexcited when you approach him, walk away immediately. Say nothing. If repeated several times over a week or so, the dog will come to learn that you release him only when he is quiet. The dog is now partly conditioned to a new set of rules that will help with visitors and family arrivals. Now we are ready for the test run.

1 Before your guest arrives or upon hearing the doorbell ring, place the lead and collar on your dog.

2 Secure the lead and collar over the hook. Don't forget to give the dog the toy stuffed with food.

3 If the dog barks incessantly, transfer him to another hook situated in another room. Ignore the dog's remonstrations.

4 Answer the door, invite your guest in, and tell them not to acknowledge your dog at all.

5 Once the dog has settled down or after about 15 minutes, let him loose but keep him on his lead for control.

6 You and the guest must not acknowledge the dog at all.

7 If the dog brings toys or uses other actions to obtain attention, ignore these too.

8 With some very badly behaved dogs, use the training disks as instructed if the dog barks when attached to his hook or when he is released from the hook.

9 Another powerful reward for behaving well is the release, but do this only when your dog is quiet.

10 If you approach your dog to release him and he begins to become overexcited, walk away as you did in the early conditioning program.

11 After a few weeks of training, calmness should be the norm. Your dog will have learned that praise, touch, and rewards are given only at your behest and when you want.

I tend to use this method until the dog willingly runs to the hook and lead upon hearing the doorbell. After a few months when I have stopped the dog from imposing on visitors, I will use the hook and lead only on occasions where I have the doors open to the street or when it's difficult to keep an eye on the dog. The hook, in some ways, is similar to a child's playpen from a safety point of view. If the psychological dominance reduction program has been used at the same time, you should by now have a much calmer and happier dog.

Below 3 and 4: The dog starts to learn that you call the shots. The use of the food toy also helps to reinforce the quiet behaviour that you want to imprint.

4

A Good Time When Tethered

Some dogs are seriously difficult or are very vocal when you restrict their movements. But they can also be helped. This is where the rubber food toy comes in. I simply fill it with a portion of their meat-based food. Always use high-quality dog food for this program. Avoid foods with lots of chemical additives as they may be influencing your dog's behavior. **Do not use dry dog foods** because they are too processed—the meat has to be sticky and of meaty texture to lodge inside the toy and be sufficiently well packed that it is difficult for your dog to extract.

If you know that guests are imminent, feed your dog that day only through the food toy. Stuff it with food, and place it in a plastic container or bag in the fridge. Your dog should have had no food prior to your visitor's arrival. Planning these training exercises in advance is critical if you are to change your dog's behavior and help him to view the hook restriction as a fun exercise.

When the guest arrives, attach the dog to his collar and lead, and place the lead loop over the hook before you invite your guest into the house. Give the food toy, stuffed with food, to your dog and answer the door, ushering your guest into the room.

Below 1, 2 and 3: When your visitor arrives and rings the door bell, restrain your dog's exuberance and attach the lead to her collar before you open the door.

Below 4: Drop the loop of the lead over the hook and give your dog the food-stuffed rubber toy to occupy her attention.

Below 5: Now you can enjoy your guest's company while also appreciating a placid dog—at last.

With repetition your dog will associate getting his food with the arrival of guests. Moreover, it will take time for him to extract the food; his mind will be concentrated on the food reward rather than trying to pester the guest. Over time, the repetition will imprint the desired behavior and your dog will become less dominant or overbearing with visitors.

Once you have reached a stage where your dog behaves calmly, accepts the food toy and food, and happily runs to his hook and lead, probably after a few months' training, it is time to dispose of the hook and use only the lead and collar and the food toy placed anywhere in your room. Bring your guest in and sit down while the dog digs into his treat. The final stages are just to place the toy on the floor while the dog is no longer tethered or on a lead. By using this approach in combination with the psychological demotion program and other methods outlined in this book, you should now have a well-behaved dog that can receive some petting when you choose to give it and that will interact with people in a calmer and more controlled way. Another benefit is that the peaceful atmosphere enables dog and owner to develop a mutual language that is clear and the dog is now able to learn new positive behaviors more willingly.

Always be attentive, however, and be aware that some dominant dogs can revert back to their old disruptive ways.

Right: A peaceful, well-controlled dog is a wonderful companion; moments like these make all the hard work worthwhile.

▶ Behavior Denied—Recap

▶ **Dashing to the front door is no longer allowed—reward removed.**

▶ **Pushing in on family or visitors is impossible to achieve—reward removed.**

▶ **Diving on people who are sitting down or demanding petting constantly is now barred—reward removed.**

▶ **Running from room to room has stopped—reward removed.**

▶ New Rewards—Recap

▶ **Being on the hook tether is now rewarded with a toy full of food.**

▶ **Being released happens only when the dog is not overexcited—the reward is being released.**

▶ **Approaching people calmly and not jumping up is rewarded with a stroke.**

▶ **Shouting and threats from annoyed people have stopped.**

▶ **Responding to obedience commands and actions produces more rewards.**

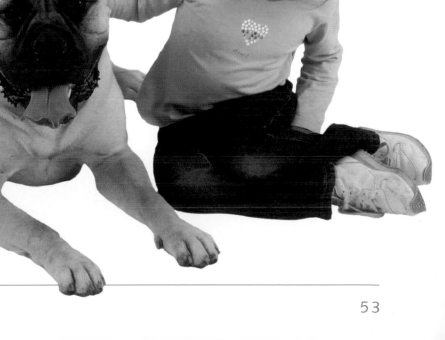

▶ Recall—Dogs That Don't Come on Command

One of the questions I am most frequently asked is how to persuade or command a dog to come when called—the exercise dog trainers term the recall. Why is it that so many people have trouble with this exercise? One answer, taking a dog's point of view, is that most owners of difficult dogs simply bore or have bored their dogs to death during walks. There is much truth in that—we ourselves would pay little attention to a family member who ignored us most of the time—but it is not the whole answer. More often than not the problem arises because we fail to understand basic canine psychology.

Let's look at it from the dog's point of view. As a dog develops from a puppy, through adolescence and into an adult dog, it explores all the marvelously varied smells in its environment, plays with all the dogs it can, and generally investigates everything that is happening in the vicinity. These pleasures are constantly reinforced by enjoyable repetition. Of course, while all this is going on, you are the last thing on your dog's mind—or rather you become just that

Above: Dogs love making friends with other dogs when out on a walk and sometimes ignore their owner's cries to come back.

if the dog has not been trained to come.

When you call your dog, it's simply a matter of whether the motivation to obey you outweighs the attractions and distractions of where the dog is at that moment—and that's the crux of the problem. Most people love letting their dogs run free in the park to play with other dogs. This is important for your dog so that he can socialize and learn how to interact with other dogs—a vital part of building up a sound temperament. But it is just as important to ensure that exploration and socialization take second place to your commands, so you have to provide the motivation for the dog to find you more interesting than

Left: Is this what happens when you call your dog back to your side during a walk? It is extremely frustrating when your cries are met with complete indifference by the dog who is much more interested in exploring the sights and smells of a new environment.

whatever else he may be doing at the moment. Not an easy task—at least for people who want to put the minimum effort into walking the dog. Another source of difficulty arises if your dog is a dominant type who wishes to make sure that all other dogs within sight are aware of his pres-

ence. This means marking territory with urine and subsequently tearing around the park pestering other dogs to assert his importance. There are other reasons for poor recall, but the methods to improve recall are the same.

Right: This is what we want—the dog returns obediently when the owner demands it. It is important to condition your dog early in his life to accept you as pack leader. Use toys and balls to make walks fun so that the dog has an incentive to come when called.

Prevention Advice

From the day you get your puppy (or, indeed, adult dog), spend time in play to capture and keep his interest. One of the simplest and most useful games to play is the retrieve, using a ball or some other favorite toy. My young dogs soon learn that I am the pack leader and the center of their world. I teach this by constantly developing games with balls, soft toys, and other chase actions. The time I put in during the first six months of ownership enables me later on to perfect the recall. The dog still enjoys play with other dogs but learns that when you command he obeys—and willingly because you are the leader and fun to return to.

Owners who fail to implant this basic idea find that in certain situations, their dogs ignore their frantic calling and that belated attempts at teaching the recall fall on deaf ears. Their dogs return to them when they are ready, not when called.

Breaking the Habit

Let's now look at some training methods to reverse this habit. It is important to remember that punishing a dog for not coming (all too often the natural human reaction) simply makes matters worse. Dogs are not inclined to come when punished, and trying to punish a dog after the event (or when you have caught it) does not allow her to make the connection between the punishment and her own actions. See the section on how dogs learn (pages 26–27).

Before deciding which training method to adopt, you need to take your own dog's character into account. For training purposes, dogs can be classed in two basic groups: the dominant and/or determined dog (DD) and the sensitive dog or puppy (SDP). Unless otherwise described, each of the training approaches considered below is suitable for both canine types. If you are unsure how to class your dog's personality, select an SDP approach first and see how you progress.

Lead and Collar Recall

Lead and collar recall is the basic system of training a dog to come. Even if you have tried and failed teaching the recall off lead, it is still best to go

Below 3 and 4: When the dog is paying attention to you, give the command "Come" and encourage the dog through your body language to approach you.

Above 1 and 2: When teaching the recall using a collar and lead, use about a 6-foot (2- m) length of lead so that the dog can move a little distance away from you initially.

Call the dog's name to gain her attention.

The dog recognizes her name and turns her head.

back to the beginning and start again with the basics of lead control and the commands "Sit," "Stay," and "Come."

Put your dog's collar on, and attach a 6-foot (2-m) lead or a retractable lead to the collar. Tell the dog to sit and stay, then walk away about 5 feet (1.5 m). Stop, do an about turn, and after a few seconds:

- Clearly call the dog's name (to gain her attention).
- Give the command "Come."
- Bend down invitingly, and when she moves toward you, offer praise as the dog nears you.
- If she doesn't come, tug on her lead and run a few steps away from her.

Then praise as she nears.

Now many of you will already have achieved this far, but the recall off lead poses greater problems. At least if your dog can achieve the above, we know she understands what we want before the next training techniques are used.

Use the command "Sit" to complete the exercise.

Reasons Why a Dog Will Not Obey You

▶ Owners have allowed the dog to find her own pleasures from puppyhood.

▶ Owners do not take on the alpha (leader) role immediately.

▶ Owners do not train the puppy to come when otherwise distracted.

▶ Owners delay the start of formal training until the puppy is too old.

▶ Owners do not teach the recall in all situations, including the home, from eight weeks.

▶ Owners select a breed that is too difficult to train in relation to their level of experience.

⑤

Above 5: Give the dog lots of verbal praise —"good dog"—and a rewarding pat when she comes back to you as commanded.

Right: Dogs respond warmly to praise from their owners. Use praise to encourage good behavior.

Sound and Food Recall

Dogs have good hearing, and most dogs enjoy eating. This method takes advantage of both these facts. If your dog isn't so keen on food, it will be more difficult, and you may need to use choice tidbits rather than regular food rations.

You'll need a dog whistle and some food. Change your dog's food to a natural, meat-based type—no dry foods. Before you start this method, introduce some time for play while you're out walking your dog—this helps to teach your dog that doing things with you can be fun. The recall training should be practiced every day for 15 minutes twice a day (perhaps while you're out walking your dog) in a quiet area with as few distractions as possible. When you feel confident and your dog begins to enjoy the training, you can progress to using an area where there are distractions present.

Do not feed the dog for one whole day. Check with your veterinarian first to make sure your dog is healthy enough to miss a meal. Begin training the next day in a quiet area, such as your yard. Divide half his normal daily food allowance into about ten portions.

Now show your dog a portion of food in your hand and run backward. As you run, give the command "Rover, come!" in an excited voice and blow the whistle once. Reward your dog with the food as soon as he comes to you. You do not need to make the dog sit at this stage. Repeat this ten times, then end the lesson. Any food you haven't used can be given to your dog on the final recall after you have attached his lead.

Above: Make sure that you call your dog on several occasions during a walk, not just when it is time to go home.

Now your dog has a real incentive to come when called, for a dog's stomach usually rules his mind. You can use the second half of his food ration for lesson two later on in the day or give him the remaining half of his meal when you return home. Continue the training for another three days, until your dog comes when you command and whistle each

Above 1: When practicing the sound and food recall, use the command "Come" and reinforce it by blowing on a dog whistle.

❶

> ### Recap
>
> ▶ **Dog learns that food arrives during walks, not at home.**
>
> ▶ **Dog learns that the new whistle sound corresponds to food rewards.**
>
> ▶ **Dog learns that the second command, "Sit," causes the delivery of instant food reward.**

time. Keep the dog on the hungry side during the first two weeks' training.

For weeks 2, 3, and 4, give your dog half his dinner (in portions) on his daily walk. Once you have him responding

quickly, use both verbal commands and the whistle. The whistle carries farther, but if you forget it, your dog needs to respond to your voice. At the end of the month we need to wean him slowly off the food.

Continue feeding your dog the remaining food (if any) in the evenings, but take two or three small portions of food with you on his walks, and use this intermittently to reinforce his recall.

Eventually, you'll need to give food rewards only occasionally—no more than once or twice a week—so your dog doesn't know when a food reward will come. However you should continue to praise your dog whenever he comes—whether it is with or without food. It requires perseverance, but it is worthwhile in the end.

Below 2 and 3: The dog has seen that you are holding a food reward and should approach you eagerly in the expectation of getting a tasty treat.

Below 4: Give the dog the tidbit as soon as she comes to you. The "Sit" command can also be given at this stage.

❷

❸

❹

It pays to keep a dog slightly hungry during the early stages of training —tidbits look even more attractive.

Below: Most dogs love a tidbit so the use of food rewards is a powerful way of imprinting good behavior and letting the dog know when she is doing the right thing.

Training Tips

▶ **Don't call your dog to put his lead on only when you are ready to go home.**

▶ **Call your dog at least ten times per walk to embed the recall (always make him sit).**

▶ **Play a game of some sort during each walk.**

▶ **If your dog is still reluctant to come when called, miss out another day of his food rations, and then try food recall again.**

The Long-Line Recall

(for determined and dominant dogs only)
This program, I feel, is one of the most successful when the handler is skilled and consistent—timing is critical. Start by obtaining a length of line, similar to curtain cord—i.e., strong and thin (many marine stores sell suitable line). You will need the line to be about 30 feet (9 m) in length. You may also find it useful to wear a gardening glove to prevent burn marks on your hand if the line should unexpectedly be pulled through your fingers. Next, tie a loop handle about six inches (15 cm) long at one end and connect

Below 1 and 2: The long-line recall technique can be practiced in open spaces where there is no danger of the line snagging an obstacle. A shorter line can even be used in the yard.

①

②

a dog clip (like the one you usually have on the end of a lead) to the other end. Attach the clip to your dog's collar, and you're ready to go.

Begin your training in a garden, yard, a quiet part of the house, or any other peaceful place with no distractions. When using the line in the garden, a shorter length, maybe 10 to 15 feet (3–4.5 m), is adequate and much easier to handle. Make sure there are no obstacles that might entangle the cord. When out in the park, avoid trees, posts, or any other objects that the line may snag on. Open grassy spaces are best.

Above: By giving a check down the line if the dog does not respond to the command "Come," you are able to attract the dog's attention at a distance.

Release your dog in your chosen area and pay out the line. If your dog runs off, simply drop the line and follow on foot (never hold the line except when checking the dog). Eventually, your dog will stop at a distraction—whether it's a tree to sniff or another dog. Now you should take hold of the trailing line at any point along its length; gather any slack and then command your dog, using his name, to "Come." If he doesn't respond, tug the line sharply to distract him. Immediately walk backward, still holding the line. If he responds and comes toward you, praise him enthusiastically. If he ignores you, repeat the command "Come," simultaneously checking him on the line until he does respond. When he arrives, tell him to sit and praise him lavishly. A small treat may also be offered.

Practice Makes Perfect

Continue to practice in the quiet place you have chosen for the first few weeks, until you have reached a standard

Below 1: Make sure that you take up any slack in the line or retractable lead before calling your dog and commanding him to "Come."

❶

Crouching down helps to gain the dog's attention.

Below 2: If the dog starts to come toward you, praise him warmly to encourage the behavior. Use a check down the line to get the attention of a dog that disobeys or gets distracted.

Keep praising the dog verbally as he comes back toward you.

whereby the dog responds to your commands without physical reinforcement.

The next stage is to practice all of the exercises in different locations, including a variety of public places.

At first he will be distracted. This is normal, but now you have to work harder. Allow the dog to run free, with the line trailing on the ground. Command "Rover, come" only, and if you get no reaction give a check down the line to interrupt, nudge, and stop the dog ignoring you. As the dog's collar is checked and he looks at you, bend low and praise him, "Clever dog," making your voice as excited as possible. Most dogs will then run toward you, at which point you should praise lavishly. It is essential not to delay the praise until the dog arrives in front of you. If the dog stops halfway, then run backward again, give the "Come" command again and reward any response with excited praise.

❷

It may take weeks to imprint the lesson, but don't give up. Repetition helps the learning process.

❸

Below 3: Mission accomplished! Make plenty of fuss of the dog when he returns to you, and perhaps give him a small tidbit as an extra reward.

Right 4: It's a great feeling when your dog willingly obeys your command to come. Excited words of encouragement and pats reinforce the message.

❹

Once the dog is at arm's length, gently take the line about three feet (1 m) from the collar and tell the dog to sit. (The line is now used like a lead.) Praise the dog for sitting and then, after about 30 seconds, release him with the command "Free," letting the line out again. Release your dog only where he can't run away. You should call your dog several times on each walk for practice. In this way, your dog won't expect to be called once only, at the end of your walk, and then attached to the lead and taken home. Also try altering your walking routine occasionally. These actions will prevent your dog anticipating when he thinks the walk will end and the usual "I don't want to come" syndrome.

The psychology of the training is this: dogs do not measure distance, so in his mind, the line could be anything from 50 to 100 yards (45 to 90 m) long. Providing you pick the line up at different lengths on different occasions, he will generally not realize that you never call him from more than the line's length away. If the dog reaches the end of the line (and providing no other distractions are nearby), I drop the line just before it tightens—the dog then trails it. The dog is not aware that I have done so. If the dog subsequently runs off say about 100 yards (90 m), I quickly catch up to the end of the line, pick it up calmly, and call him. If he comes immediately, I praise him and run backward. If he ignores me, I give a sharp check down the line.

Dealing with Distractions

The dog may find various distractions more interesting than you or what you are trying to teach him. This is when a number of owners give up, because their dog may appear to be regressing. This is not the case! The dog is simply making choices based on past experiences that were generally in his favor.

The dog does not forget what you have taught him but instantly associates your command with either your positive enforcement of obedience, or your lack of it, in the past. You want your dog to be obedient in all circumstances. **Do not give up—continue!** Within a few days of consistent reinforcement, the dog will respond to your commands.

When you are training in a public place, other dogs may run up to you and your dog. Their intentions may be friendly, or their owners may have little or no control over them. Under these circumstances, especially in the first few weeks of training, it is best to heel your dog off briskly to another area. In difficult circumstances, I simply connect the lead to the dog's collar and disconnect the line, leaving it on the ground to pick up a few minutes later. This avoids entanglements—especially if you have someone else's uncontrollable and boisterous dog around you. Your dog cannot be expected to learn while other dogs are jumping all over him. There is also a danger of the line getting caught

Below 1: It is almost inevitable when you are teaching your dog long-line recall in a public place that other dogs will come on the scene and very possibly cause a distraction that will interfere with your training.

Below 2: The other dog is probably just being inquisitive, but it is hard to gain your dog's attention in such circumstances.

1

2

Below 1: Always praise your dog as he comes obediently toward you on command.

Below 2 and 3: A stroke and a "good dog" show that you are pleased. Then command your dog to "Sit" and again praise him when he obeys you.

around both of the dogs, and this situation should be avoided.

Line training works well on most dogs. The only exception is very large dogs that aren't sensitive to being checked unless you use excessive force, which is not recommended.

Recap

▶ **Your dog learns that when he ignores you a check comes down the line.**

▶ **Running backward as you call him encourages a dog to come to you.**

▶ **As the dog runs to you and when he reaches you, praise him, then give the command "Sit" and more praise. A treat may also be a pleasant reward for coming when called.**

▶ **When the dog runs to you, act pleased—and interested.**

Below 3: The best course of action is to call your dog to heel and head off to a quieter part of the park.

Right: It is important for puppies to socialize with other older dogs, but they do get in the way of training exercises and are liable to cause distractions in the early stages of training.

Sound and Toy Recall

Dogs have good hearing, and most dogs enjoy playing with a favorite toy; this method utilizes both these facts. However, if your dog isn't so keen on toys, then first you will have to teach the Long-line Recall (see above) before following these instructions further.

You'll need a dog whistle, as in the long-line training, and a toy (ball, squeaky toy, etc.). Start by removing all toys from the house and placing them in a secure cupboard. Select a favorite toy, and take it with you on your walk to begin training the same day in a quiet area you have chosen.

Now show your dog the toy in your hand and run backward, simultaneously and excitedly commanding: "Rover, come!" and waving the toy in the air in an excited manner. Reward your dog by throwing the toy once and allowing him to retrieve and give it back to you (use a long line or lead trailing if your dog refuses to bring it back). Repeat this ten times, then end the lesson. Throw the toy for your dog on the final recall, then attach his lead and head home.

Now your dog has a real incentive to come when called, for a dog's motivation to retrieve and participate in interaction with the owner normally overrules his desire to follow other distractions. When you return home, make sure no toys are available to the dog, with **no exceptions**.

Continue the training for another three days until your dog comes on command each time, using the toy method.

For a further month, continue this routine on his daily walk. Once the dog responds instantly, try keeping the toy out of sight until the dog comes right up to you. Drop the verbal commands

Lock away all toys at home so that the dog will get extra enjoyment out of playtime in the park.

Above 1 -4: You can use the fact that most dogs love retrieval games to your advantage when teaching recall. When the dog obeys your command to "Come" and the associated whistle signal, he is rewarded with a fun game of fetch the toy.

③ **④**

This lesson can be repeated up to ten times on a walk. Then allow the dog one final fetch before heading home.

▶ Sound and Toy Recall—Recap

▶ Dog learns that toys are available only during walks, not at home.

▶ Dog learns that coming when called is rewarded by an exciting game.

▶ Toy reward is gradually phased out, but reward of praise continues.

▶ Any item that encourages a dog to come to you can be used.

❶

and use the whistle only—although you may praise him as he runs toward you. At the end of the month, we need to wean him slowly off the toy, so use it to reinforce his recall intermittently.

Eventually, you'll need to throw the toy reward only occasionally so your dog doesn't know when the rewarding game will come. When I say occasionally, I mean no more than once or twice a walk. However, you should continue to praise your dog at all times when he comes, whether it's with or without the toy. It does require perseverance.

Below 1, 2, and 3: Once the dog has learned the lesson that coming when called is rewarded with a game, you should gradually phase out the use of the toy but keep praising him for being obedient.

❷

❸

Hide-and-Seek Recall

Dogs are pack animals and, though your dog may not come back on command, he will still generally keep you in view—even at great distances. This method manipulates your dog's natural instinct to stay with the pack.

Take your dog out to a large fenced area with plenty of hiding places. Release him where there are few dogs, and quickly run off and hide. Let your dog see you hide. Many dogs quickly run to you, both out of curiosity and pack instinct. A few don't seem to care. When you are discovered, offer a treat like ham pieces or a favorite toy, so the dog has a reward for coming, and give him plenty of dramatic and excited praise. Over a period of weeks, keep hiding, but gradually make it more difficult for the dog to find you.

Without the recall command being issued, I have found that most dogs actually become acutely attentive to your location and by default listen and begin to come on command.

Citronella Collar Recall

(for determined and dominant dogs only)
The citronella collar is another innovative electronic device that is remote controlled. When used with knowledge—an important factor—it is excellent in teaching DD dogs the recall. It works on the same training psychology as the long line except that the line is replaced by the remote-controlled collar. The battery-powered collar is filled with a citronella liquid, which is harmless to dogs. When the hand device is depressed, a jet of citronella spray is released from the collar beneath the dog's chin, forming a cloud of vapor in front of the dog's nose. This has two possible results:
• The sudden, strong-smelling spray alarms the dog, who escapes back to an owner who is happily calling to the dog.
• The dog's play or investigation is abruptly interrupted, giving her the opportunity to hear and respond to the "Come" command once more.

For the dog, it's an unpleasant experience to be startled by a sudden burst of citronella if she ignores her owner's commands. Most dogs decide that the best reaction is to run to their owners for attention or support. You can then complete the recall exercise. The dog does not associate the unpleasant experience she had over there with you standing over here. However, she quickly associates coming to you with praise and a tidbit. It is essential that you fully understand timing in dog training before using the citronella collar. See the section on timing in Chapter 1 How Dogs Learn before employing this method.

Try to avoid calling the dog if you are unable to reinforce the command, even if that means that the dog goes where you may not wish her to. In this way, the dog does not have the opportunity to disobey your command—so she does not learn that disobedience is an option.

Above 1: The citronella collar can be remotely activated by pressing a button on the small hand controller, which transmits a signal to the collar.

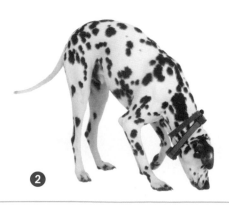

Below 2: The collar emits a cloud of bitter-smelling spray that startles the dog.

Reinforcers

▶ **Favorite tidbits—I recommend chicken or ham pieces.**

▶ **Favorite toys, balls, etc. Don't give the toys to the dog at any other time except during training. Take all toys home and lock them away.**

▶ **The pleasure of playing a game with you.**

▶ **The dog's daily dinner given in portions as a reward.**

❶

❷

Above 1: There are various reinforcers that you can use to encourage good behavior. Tidbits and retrieve games played with toys or balls are all rewarding for the puppy or dog.

Above 2: If you plan to use toys as part of the recall training program, lock them away at home so that the dog can enjoy playing with them only on your terms.

Right 3: The dog will normally stop what he is doing and either return to you for reassurance or be attentive to your command to "Come."

Right: It's a pleasure for all the family to go for a walk with a dog that will come back reliably to your side when called. Training does require patience, but persistence should pay dividends.

Remember to praise your dog when he comes on your call.

❸

▶ Separation Anxiety—Home Alone

Dogs and people love each other's company, and that is the reason most of us have dogs. Indeed, dogs often become more inextricably linked with our lives than we realize. Like their cousins, wolves, dogs are gregarious by nature and unsuited to leading solitary lives. That's almost certainly why we get on so well with them. From a dog's point of view, we are the family pack, and so, whether he lives with one person or a large family, he instinctively enjoys, and needs, our company. Leaving a dog alone regularly for long periods is not kind and does not equate with responsible dog ownership. However, like wolves and indeed humans, dogs can adapt to spending reasonable stretches of time in their own company without suffering severe psychological problems.

For most well-adjusted dogs, anxieties rarely develop to the point of causing problem behavior. However, some dog owners find that leaving their beloved pet dog for even a short time can result in the most extraordinary behavior, and this is what I shall explore in this chapter. Reactions to being left alone can take many forms including barking, howling, self-mutilation, excessively boisterous behavior on the owner's return, destructiveness, and even biting the owner as he or she leaves the house. All are caused by stress and come under the heading of separation anxiety.

This can be a severe problem, as in a Golden Retriever bitch I dealt with that nipped several family members as they were about to leave the house in the morning (combining separation anxiety with a touch of dominance aggression). A Labrador owner recalled how her dog just wandered off to her son's bedroom when left alone and chewed through two pairs of handmade leather shoes. Leather is an attractive chewing material to many anxious dogs. It can be a comforter—in the same way that some people binge on chocolate when feeling down. The fact is that dogs do chew when they are puppies—that's normal

Below 1 and 2: *Dogs and humans get along well together—that's why we value their company and let them share our homes.*

❶

❷

canine behavior. We become understandably upset when our treasured goods are damaged—that's normal human behavior. However, if we, as owners, try to understand our dog's needs and general behavior, most of the unpleasant circumstances that I have described are avoidable.

3

4

Left and above 3 and 4:
Displays of destructiveness while
left alone such as this are typical
of dogs that suffer from separation
anxiety. More definite signs include
destruction around doors and
windows, urination, defecation,
salivation, barking, howling, and
panting.

Right: "Please...
I don't want to
be alone."

The dog has realized that he is about
to be left on his own.

Dogs are
remarkably
sensitive to the
warning signs that
you are about to
leave, such as
picking up house
keys or putting
on a coat.

Signs of Separation Anxiety

**When you prepare to leave
the house, your dog**

▶ **paces to and fro**

▶ **salivates heavily**

▶ **barks**

▶ **nips your clothes**

▶ **acts excitedly**

**When you return, your
dog has**

▶ **defecated or urinated**

▶ **chewed or licked himself sore**

▶ **barked and howled**

▶ **been destructive, especially
around doors or windows**

• **The dog may exhibit any one or more of these symptoms.**

General Causes

This problem nearly always arises when a puppy is spoiled or not conditioned to accept an appropriate routine. As a youngster, he may have been allowed to sleep in his owner's bedroom and received constant attention, or his cute and cuddly appearance may have attracted excessive fussing from visitors and family alike. The unwitting result can be a dog that thinks he has a right to demand attention whenever he wishes and that this is normal behavior. So if you respond to a dog every time he blinks his doleful eyes at you, you could have a separation anxiety problem in the making. Often I describe these dogs as helpless when alone. The bottom line is that we actually cause the problem ourselves by misguided acts of kindness.

Dogs that literally go everywhere with their owner, day and night, can also turn out to be owner dependent. Understandably, therefore, separation anxiety is more common in single-person households, especially when elderly people live alone with a dog as their sole companion. If only you and the dog occupy a house, then naturally you will be together most of the time. But there are measures you can take to teach your dog to be self-sufficient without forfeiting a close and rewarding relationship.

Dogs that are nervous or great natural attention seekers may receive or solicit extra care and attention from sensitive owners in their early years, causing an excessively close bond and over-dependency.

A sudden reduction in the amount of time and attention you give your dog may well upset him. For example, a dog that has been tenderly nursed through an illness may become distressed when he recovers and the extra fuss suddenly stops. Of course, dogs' personalities vary, so another dog may take this situation in her stride with little or no change in her behavior. Again, a sudden change in the owner's lifestyle—for example, if an owner who has previously been at home all day takes up a job outside the home—will affect the dog. A highly dependent dog will find it most difficult to be alone without the normal company of a family member.

Are You the Problem?

I would argue that dogs are blameless and that we are always the problem. I have been dealing with dogs and their owners for very many years, and this has taught me a great deal about canine-human relationships and the complex ways that we condition our dogs for our own psychological comfort and needs. We are usually not aware of this, but in some cases, this interdependence can develop to an unhealthy level. If circumstances change suddenly—for example, if we acquire a new partner or a different job—and the dog is no longer needed as much, then he may react badly and develop separation anxiety.

Insecure dogs often want attention and company on demand, which compounds the separation anxiety problem. When you comply with your dog's demands, he comes to expect attention every time he asks, until the habit becomes

Left: People who live alone with only a dog for company naturally forge very close ties with their pets. However, excessive pampering can create a situation where the dog becomes totally reliant on her owner's company.

Right: Children love showering attention on their cuddly pets. But if circumstances change—the children disappear to school all day, for instance—the dog can become unsettled, missing all the fuss that he craves.

firmly embedded. When there isn't enough attention, i.e, when you are not around, then separation anxiety may occur. You may observe excessive excitability and even shaking and shivering prior to your leaving, and, once you've gone, barking and destruction may follow. Barking is probably the most common sign of separation anxiety, probably because in itself it produces some emotional relief, perhaps through the release of endorphins.

Below: Barking is a common symptom of separation anxiety—not good for you, the dog, or neighborly relations.

Causes in Brief

▸ **Dogs have not learned from puppyhood to spend time alone but are given free run of the home with human company in all rooms.**

▸ **Some owners coddle their dogs excessively, often to satisfy their own emotional needs, thereby teaching the dogs to be helpless.**

▸ **Some dogs learn to be wholly human oriented, ignoring their own kind, which causes imbalance and insecurity.**

▸ **Small, cuddly breeds tend to attract excessive human attention, so separation anxiety is more common among toy breeds.**

Prevention Advice

The ideal solution is prevention, so I'll cover that first. If you have a puppy or a new dog, then teach her that it is normal to be left alone for periods of half an hour to an hour several times a day—and for longer at night. This should be done gradually, starting with five minutes per session. It is of course much easier with a puppy than with an adult dog. Teach your puppy that she has her own area (or pen or cage) where you will visit her. Do not give the dog access to your whole house. If the puppy starts to cry when she's alone in her pen, wait until a silence occurs, then go in and make a mild fuss, but not too much, otherwise you may encourage separation anxiety. Don't let the dog think that every time you come to her area she will be let out; sometimes leave the dog in and sometimes let her out. In other words, be unpredictable in order to avoid setting up expectations.

With an attention-seeking dog, many people fall into the trap of patting her whenever she solicits affection. When they think they've shown her enough attention, they stop and expect their dog to understand that they've been fair. What they don't realize is that the dog has no concept of fairness. All she knows is that if she persists, she can obtain the attention she wants. This only serves to reinforce the dog's dependency on (and/or dominance over) the owner.

Dealing with Separation Anxiety— Reducing Dependence

If possible, start this program during a long holiday weekend. Begin by reducing the amount of attention your dog receives during a 24-hour period to 25 percent of what it was. Ignore all the dog's attempts to solicit attention, whether by nudging you,

"I wonder if he'll stroke me?"

❶

bringing toys, or looking pleadingly for a pat. You'll find this hard at first, but you and all your family and friends must be consistent.

Next, start leaving your dog on her own in a room of the house for periods of five minutes while you are still in the house. If the dog begins to cry or bark or sound excited, don't go into the room. When a gap in the barking comes, wait 30 seconds, then go in casually, saying nothing and keeping the contact low-key. On no account should bursts of excitement from the dog be reciprocated. Then putter about for a few minutes and let the dog go free in the house. Ensure that no one pats the dog, no matter how

Left: Try to accustom a dog from puppyhood that it's normal to spend periods of time on her own. The use of an indoor cage is helpful when doing this.

A pat or stroke signals a small victory for the dog. Remain aloof instead.

over several weeks, then you'll have a greater chance of success. But it is important that the regimen continues.

You can combine this method with the next one by giving the dog a part of her dinner via a specially designed food-stuffed rubber toy (explained below) when she is on her own in the kitchen. This means that the dog is actually rewarded for being out of your company. Your dog should also receive her toys and food when not in your company. In other words, be as boring as you can possibly be when the dog is with you.

Below: This dog feels insecure. By following the dependence reduction program, the dog will come to accept time spent without you.

Above 1, 2, and 3: When you are working with your dog to reduce its sense of dependence on you, avoid the temptation to pat it whenever it pesters you. Use the Ignore response instead.

Above: The toy-fetching routine is another tactic to gain your attention. It may seem hard-hearted, but you must ignore the bait that the dog is desperate that you take.

much she solicits praise. The dog's initial puzzlement or even worse behavior will soon give way to acceptance of the new arrangements after a few days.

If this regimen is adhered to, it slowly teaches the dog that it's no great deal to be with you or without you. You should aim to leave your dog alone for five-minute periods, working up to four to six times a day. When this is achieved without any commotion, then slowly begin increasing the period your dog spends alone up to the desired time to fit in with your social patterns. If you introduce this program gradually

The Use of Food

Using food rewards to modify your dog's behavior produces positive associations with your absence. The most useful aid is a tough rubber toy designed to be stuffed with food, which the dog has to pull out bit by bit. Instead of gulping his dinner down in a flash, he has a time-consuming but rewarding new hobby.

- Keep your dog in the kitchen area when you are out.
- Use a sticky food that the dog must work at to get out.
- Feed your dog his daily dinner only through the toy.
- If you are out three times in one day, split the day's ration into three portions.
- Use the toy, and stuff it with food when you are about to leave your dog.
- Place the toy on the kitchen floor, and let the dog work on extracting the food each time it is placed on the floor.
- You can still use this method even if you are not going out. Leave the dog in the kitchen three times daily for about 15 minutes, and each time leave him the toy with a portion of his dinner inside. This will accustom the dog to positive rewards when you are out of the room, even though you may still be present in the house.
- Do not feed your dog or give him tidbits at any other time. All food must be fed through the toy.
- If your dog does not consume the food in the toy, place the whole thing in a plastic container in the fridge until the next lesson. Very few dogs will ignore the food in the toy by the second day.

Below: *When it is time to go out and leave your dog alone at home, consider using food as a diversionary tactic to keep his mind off being on his own.*

The combination of the two methods described had a 95 percent success rate last year at my center with dogs from a wide range of breeds suffering from separation anxiety.

The dog is totally absorbed in getting at the food.

①

②

③

④

Above 1, 2, 3, and 4: The beauty of the toy stuffed with food is that the dog really has to work at it to extract the food. While he is concentrating on it, nosing it around on the floor and trapping it with his paws, the fact that you are out of the room is forgotten.

The food that you use in the toy should be meaty and moist—dry food will not work. By cramming it into the toy and compressing it, you create a diversion that occupies the dog's attention and rewards his persistence with food.

Two's Canine Company

Another way to occupy your dog during your absence is to see if a friend's or neighbor's dog can keep him company. You need to make sure it is a dog that gets on well with yours and that they are left somewhere they can play without wrecking anything. The best combination is usually a male and a female. However, this method will not work if your dog is specifically over-attached to you personally and does not like playing with other dogs.

Below: Another simple ploy to deal with separation anxiety is to arrange for your dog to enjoy the company of another while you are out.

Above: Introduce your dog to the food toy by giving him his daily food ration through a toy placed on the kitchen floor in place of a conventional food bowl.

Exercise the Energy

Try lengthening your dog's exercise periods prior to leaving him alone, and make more effort to tire him out. Throw a ball and run around or let your dog play with other friendly dogs. Don't just go for a lethargic stroll. Then when you arrive home, leave your dog on his own for a while. If he's tired, he's much more likely to settle down and go to sleep. As in the previous method, gradually build up the time that you leave your dog alone.

During walks and exercise, you can praise and touch your dog as much as you like, especially when obedience training him. While you are working on dealing with separation anxiety, you will usually find as a bonus that your dog becomes far more obedient about the house and in the park.

Important Tips

1 Do not allow your dog to decide when attention should be forthcoming. Let any attention be on your terms. You decide when enough is enough. So for the next few months always ignore your dog if he requests attention.

2 If the anxiety is triggered by your leaving the house, then pretend to leave several times a day. Go through all the motions, including putting on your coat and going to your car. With so many false starts to contend with, your dog won't be able to predict when you are leaving, and this should disrupt the ingrained anxiety behavior.

3 Whenever you return home or when your dog has been in another room on his own for a while, don't greet him effusively or overexcite him. Instead, adopt a low-key approach. In this way, your dog will not look

❶

Below 1, 2, 3, and 4: Dogs may start to show signs of anxiety when they anticipate that you are about to leave the house. By making a number of "false starts" throughout the day, you can confuse the dog's expectations and so reduce her anxiety.

Are you going out or not? The dog is no longer sure what this routine is leading up to.

❶   ❷   ❸

When the training has paid off and the dog's anxiety has been reduced, strokes and pats can be returned to the menu.

Above 1, 2, and 3: When a dog jumps up to pester for attention, avoid eye contact, don't offer any pats, and, if necessary, stand up to force her to get down again.

For all the dog knows, you may turn around and come straight back. What's there to worry about?

upon your return as a big deal. Better still, ignore the dog completely for the first five minutes.

4 Remember that many dogs that crave attention consider being pushed off or reprimanded as a form of reward. So simply stand upright with your hands at your side if your dog jumps on you. Pause, then sit down again. Repeat until the dog loses interest. Don't give the dog any eye contact.

In Conclusion

I have found that most dogs respond well to the above methods and that eventually you can reinstate a moderate amount of affectionate response—in other words a relationship that both of you still enjoy. However, a few dogs are so conditioned to effusive displays of affection from their owners that praise and fuss always have to be kept to a minimum to prevent the dog's anxiety becoming unbearable again.

Recap

▸ **Teach your dog to be alone, initially for short periods.**

▸ **Use food rewards (the daily ration given via the food-stuffed toy) so the dog develops pleasant associations with separation from you.**

▸ **Tidbits given at other times are not helpful in solving this problem.**

▸ **Some dogs like chew bones, but swallowing rawhide can be dangerous.**

▸ **Don't allow your dog treats (including toys) when in your company, except when out on walks.**

Excessive Barking

For dogs, barking is a natural form of communication, and they do it for innumerable reasons. A dog would hardly be a dog if he didn't bark sometimes. However, when barking becomes prolonged or excessive, it can be a problem. Strangely enough, the dog's ancestor, the wolf, rarely barks. Howling is his forte—it is a way of transmitting messages to others of its kind.

There are several reasons for excessive barking or howling. Some owners encourage a puppy to bark to develop her guarding ability. In other cases, the owners have unintentionally encouraged her to bark from puppyhood. Whenever the dog barked, her owners appeared and gave her attention. Finding this behavior rewarding, the dog quite naturally continued to bark more and more. This is especially true of puppies.

Some dogs bark from stress when separated from their owners. Others bark from boredom when they don't

Right: We expect dogs to bark when the doorbell rings—in fact it is useful to be alerted to people approaching the house. But when the barking goes on and on, the behavior becomes unacceptable.

Prevention Advice for Puppies

The ideal solution is prevention. If you have a puppy or a new dog, teach her that it's normal to be left alone for periods of half an hour to an hour several

have enough stimulation. A dog whose routine is changed so that its owner can't spend as much time with her as usual may become frustrated and anxious—this is another cause of excessive barking or related problem behavior.

Above 1, 2, 3, and 4: This dog is mooching around aimlessly and generally giving the impression of being thoroughly bored. In situations where they lack stimulation, some dogs take to prolonged sessions of barking as a way of relieving their boredom.

times a day and for longer at night. This should be done gradually, starting with five- to ten-minute periods.

Also teach your puppy that she has her own cage, pen, or area where you will visit her. Don't, as a norm, give her

❶ ❷ ❸ ❹

A dog must learn to be on his own.

access to your whole house. If, while the puppy is alone in her pen, she starts to cry, then wait until a silence occurs before going in and making a mild fuss over her. Verbal praise is sufficient, but not too much—otherwise you may encourage the barking.

It is natural for dogs to bark when visitors knock or ring the doorbell. Most owners don't mind this—territorial guarding is natural dog behavior. But don't let the dog overdo it, otherwise you could end up with an excessive barker. Most dogs that drive their owners mad by barking at the door were taught when to bark but not when to stop.

Barking While the Owner Is Home

Some dogs don't like being left alone in the yard or in an adjacent room and as a result bark until the owner attends to their needs, which normally means giving the dog access to human company again. What a powerful reward! No wonder dogs learn to bark. If your dog is this type of barker, then follow the dominance reduction and Ignore programs (see pages 28–29, 44–45), and read the section on separation anxiety-related barking (see pages 72–73) for more advice.

①

Get the dog used to spending time in the cage.

②

③

Above 1, 2, and 3: Dogs that have become accustomed to spending lots of time with their owners during puppyhood may resort to barking later in their lives when they are left on their own. A good way of preventing this problem developing is to teach the dog during his formative months that it is normal to spend time alone in a cage, pen, or kennel away from the rest of the family.

How to Stop or Reduce Barking

Programs to reduce barking when left alone are similar to those designed to treat separation anxiety, except that the emphasis is on simply reducing barking. Begin by reducing the amount of attention the dog receives during a 24-hour period, ignoring all the dog's attempts to solicit attention. You'll find this hard at first, but you must be consistent.

Then leave the dog by herself in a room of the house for periods of five minutes while you're still at home. If the dog begins to bark, do not go into the room. When a gap in the barking comes, wait 30 seconds, then nonchalantly wander in and say hello, but keep the praise low key. On no account should bursts of excitement from the dog be reciprocated. Then putter about for a few minutes and let the dog go free in the house. Ensure that no one pets the dog, no matter how much she solicits

praise. The dog must not view being with you as a right, or associate it with a reward, such as touch, praise, etc.

Adhering to this regimen slowly teaches the dog that it's no great deal to be with you or without you. You should aim to leave your dog alone for five- to 15-minute periods five times daily. When this is achieved without barking, then slowly begin increasing the period that your dog spends alone, building up to the desired time. The longer you spread the program, the more chance you have of success. Alternatively, you can condition the dog to enjoy being away from you through using its food.

Warning
Except in exceptional circumstances, dogs should not be left on their own for an entire day.

Left: This training program relies on you significantly reducing the amount of attention that you grant your dog.

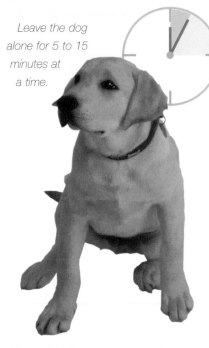

Leave the dog alone for 5 to 15 minutes at a time.

Above: *The key to stopping a dog that persistently barks when she is left on her own is to accustom her gradually to spending short periods of time alone several times a day.*

Above: Don't respond or visit your dog while she is barking—reward her silence, not her demands for attention.

Anxiety-Related Barking

Many dogs are overattached to their owners and appear to be incapable of spending time on their own. Use the following methods on such dogs to change their view of spending time alone. It is normal in human society for people to spend time alone even though we are a gregarious species. Wolf society is also pack oriented, but wolves can and do spend time alone, and domestic dogs are equally equipped to adapt to being on their own. There are several approaches we can use to help them do so.

Food Inducement

Food is on a dog's mind most of the time, and if it's not, then we can easily induce them to think food, or at least make dinnertime more exciting. Always use high-quality food for this program.

▶ Dealing with Fussy Eaters

▶ Most dogs learn to be fussy eaters through their owner's actions, when food refusal is rewarded by the substitution of tastier food. Dogs that are known fussy eaters should go a full day without food before you begin training, to increase their natural hunger pangs. Consult your veterinarian first, however. Some cases labeled as fussiness can be signs of medical problems. Not all dogs can cope with missing meals. Do not restrict eating practices if the dog is old or unwell.

Above: The food-filled rubber toy described in Chapter 2 is a powerful training aid. Instead of barking when alone, dogs learn to anticipate the reward of a food treat.

Avoid generic or unbalanced diets, which might influence your dog's health and behavior.

You will need a tough rubber toy designed to be stuffed with food (see Training Aids). For the next five weeks, your dog will receive his daily food intake only through the toy and in your absence. Divide his day's ration into five portions to stuff into the toy. If he ignores the food in the toy, simply place the whole thing in a plastic container back in the fridge until the next lesson.

If the dog eats the food willingly, he will have learned to do so in your absence and will associate your absence with a powerful food reward that takes time to extract. He is being rewarded for being separated from you. If he barks, he can't eat and you must ignore him. Enter the dog's room only when he is silent. He must not associate his barking activities with your arrival. Remember—**no tidbits or food at any other time!**

Helpful Distractions

Some trainers recommend leaving a radio on while you're out to keep the dog company. This works in a few cases. Even more effective is the use of a tape recorder to play back the sound of your own voice to the dog while you are away.

Some dogs that bark when left alone can be distracted by leaving them food treats or a favorite toy to keep them busy until your return. You will need to prevent access to toys and chews when you're at home so that they become a special treat associated with your absence.

Excitable Barking for Attention

This type of barking can be a social nuisance when it gets excessive. The way to deal with it is by using counter-conditioning. For example, if the dog barks when he sees you eating, stop feeding the dog by hand and give him food only in his bowl. Don't allow the dog any food reward if he stares or barks at you. Employ the Ignore program (see pages 28–29). Better still, don't allow the dog in your presence when eating.

If your dog reacts with boisterous barking when you take the car keys or pick up his lead and collar or your coat, then simply confuse the dog's ability to anticipate your actions.

Above: His Master's Voice? The sound of a radio playing quietly in the background, or even a tape recording of your voice, can help some dogs to become used to spending time on their own without resorting to fits of barking.

Play is a great way of stopping a dog getting bored when she is left on her own.

This is done by altering walk times whenever possible, picking up the aforementioned articles 5 or 10 times a day, or even putting on your coat and walking to the front door only to return to your sofa. This saturates the dog with so many false starts not leading to the expected result that (unless he's really stupid) the message will get through.

Never shout or scream at the barking dog to shut up, as this often increases the atmosphere of excitement as far as

Below: Food chews can keep dogs happy for hours while their owners are out of the house.

Recap

▷ **Don't reward bad behavior.**

▷ **Confuse the cues that elicit barking.**

▷ **Keep calm—shouting only adds to the excitement.**

▷ **Remember: dogs bark naturally, but they learn to bark excessively only when we owners unwittingly reinforce this behavior.**

  ▷ **Interrupt the barking by throwing training disks near the dog at the time of barking only.**

Above: Toys help a dog to enjoy time spent alone, although not many dogs know how to skateboard!

Left: If your dog barks when you put on your coat for a walk, confuse her expectations by making repeated false starts. Walk to the door, stop, and return to the front room again.

Above: Some dogs start barking when they see their owners eating in anticipation of the reward of a tidbit from their hands. In such cases, only feed the dog through her own bowl and don't give any tidbits or rewards while you are eating.

the dog's concerned, "My owner grabs my lead, I bark wildly, my owner shouts with me, I jump up and down, my owner waves his arms at me: oh, isn't it fun!"

Training disks, when properly introduced, are a very effective means of stopping this type of behavior in attention-seeking, dominant, boisterous dogs. While the dog is barking, throw the disks (or a large bunch of keys) near the dog so that the sound startles him into silence. When your dog stops barking, don't make a fuss of him and stoke the excitement up again. Wait impassively for a minute of silence, then limit your praise to a softly spoken "Good dog."

Barking Mad in the Car

Most dogs love cars and all the accompanying excitement of going for a drive. They associate cars with fun—being with you, going on a hunt, a walk in the park. Riding in the car has all the visual stimulus of a hunt, with other dogs and animals flashing by. Dogs that express this excitement by barking nonstop in the car are a big problem for many people. Prolonged or excessive barking is aggravating, and when it occurs right in your ear while you are driving, it can be dangerous. Many a driver has had an accident while trying to quieten a dog in a car, normally in anger.

Using Deterrents

More sensitive dogs, and dogs that are caught in the developing stages of the barking habit, may respond well to spray deterrents. When traveling, take a water pistol. When your dog starts to bark, squirt the water in her face, simultaneously giving the command "No" in a firm voice. Don't raise your voice, or the dog will think you are joining in and take this as encouragement to bark!

Alternatively, you can use a commercially produced deterrent spray that squirts a fine mist of harmless but very bitter liquid into the air. It's difficult for a dog to bark while inhaling such a pungent smell. By the way, you won't like the smell either! You can also buy a special remote-activated collar that squirts citronella spray when the dog barks, but this should be used only with the expert help of a trainer, as some dogs are very sensitive to the jet spray or

accompanying sound. Alternatively, you could use the training disks as outlined in Chapter 2. For safety reasons, it is best to have a friend sitting next to you on car journeys to apply the deterrent for the first four or five sessions and occasionally thereafter.

If you are consistent, most dogs will find the experience distracting and unpleasant. As soon as you have 30 seconds of silence, quietly praise your dog verbally in a low key voice. Don't stroke him or make a fuss of him, as this will simply re-excite him. Your dog should learn that silence brings pleasant praise

Above and left: A food-filled toy (left) is a useful distraction—it occupies the mind of a persistent barker who might otherwise be creating mayhem in the car. If your dog shows destructive tendencies when left alone in the car, try confining him in a travel cage or behind a dog guard (above).

as a reward and that barking means trouble. I also find that placing a food-stuffed toy in the car serves as a pleasant distraction for the less serious cases.

Redesigning the Car Space

Some dogs suffer from separation anxiety when left in the car. They may take out their frustration on the car interior or simply attempt to escape, chewing and scratching and causing damage that

---

> ## Training Equipment to Tackle Barking
>
> ▸ **Training disks—thrown near dog.**
>
> ▸ **Water pistol—squirted at dog.**
>
> ▸ **Deterrent spray—squirted in the air near dog's head.**
>
> ▸ **Remote-activated spray collar (under expert supervision only).**

Below 1 and 2: As the pictures show, this is not a training method to use if you are driving a vehicle on your own. Instead, ask a friend to accompany you on a car journey while your dog is restrained by a travel harness in the back. If he starts to bark, your friend can throw the disks while commanding "No." When the dog falls silent, quietly say a few words of praise.

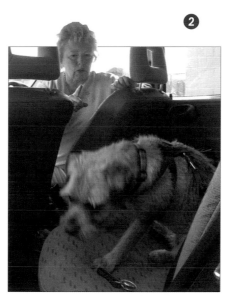

dog and give a food reward. Repeat this process several times daily for a week. In the second week, begin to walk the dog around your yard or living room on a lead and head collar. During the third week, progress to walking your dog short distances to and from the car, again using food rewards.

Finally, place the dog, fitted with head collar and lead, in the car. The lead should be about four feet (1.2 m) long and made of nylon or leather. Connect it to a fixture in the car, leaving the dog room to sit and lie down only. Unable to jump about wildly, the dog will become calmer and less prone to bark.

Car harnesses especially made for dogs are also helpful for restraining wild movements and stop dogs jumping to and fro as they work themselves up into a barking frenzy.

may be quite extensive. Owners of such dogs will find that the use of a traveling cage fitted in the car not only keeps the dog safe en route but enables you to keep your car interior in good condition. Accustom your dog to the cage first (see page 173), and tie the cage down securely.

Restraints

Alternatively, it is worth trying a head collar, which has a calming and controlling effect on most dogs. Head collars are made in various styles and sizes to fit most breeds. Initially, many dogs dislike wearing them (as with all muzzles and collars). Accustom your dog to the head collar gradually by fitting her for a few minutes each day in the home. Make the dog sit, using a lead attached to the head collar, then immediately praise the

Summary

▷ **Nip the barking habit in the bud—don't let it build up into a big problem.**

▷ **Reward silence, not barking.**

▷ **Have a helper in the car initially.**

▷ **A squirt in time teaches silence.**

▷ **Consider the use of a dog guard or traveling cage in the car.**

▷ **Accustom your dog to a harness or head collar.**

▷ **Don't shout.**

It's natural for dogs to bark, but don't let the habit get out of hand.

Excessive Attention Seeking

Attention seeking—what does this actually mean? After all, most dogs are "show-offs" who love attention. Dogs wouldn't be dogs unless they did. In fact, dogs that seek our attention are the most trainable, and trainers develop a host of methods to attract a dog's attention in order to teach obedience and general sociable manners. However, when the attention-seeking dog interferes with your lifestyle or stops you from getting on with your daily chores, then this behavior becomes unacceptable.

This problem is often caused by over-indulging the dog in puppyhood. It is easy for a cute puppy to attract a lot of attention and all too easy to produce a dog that thinks she has a right to demand attention whenever she wishes. Dogs that go everywhere with their owners,

Above: *It is easy to fall under the spell of puppies and small dogs and to indulge their whims whenever they want attention. But it not always a good idea, as the dog may start to view such attention as her right.*

Above: *Mothers with young babies have incredibly busy lifestyles with plenty to occupy them throughout the day. What they don't need is an attention-seeking dog that butts in and interferes with the daily routine in the house.*

day and night, can also turn out to be excessive attention seekers, though more often than not they develop separation anxiety, another common behavioral problem.

Excessive attention seeking is typical of the dominant dog (see Chapter 3). However, in this chapter we will simply look at methods of tackling this problem on its own, rather than introducing the complete retraining program for dominant dogs, which might be too drastic a solution for many dog owners.

Symptoms

- ► • **Jumping up on your lap**
- ► • **Pushing in**
- ► • **Constant nudging**
- ► • **Barking**

The Doggy Drive

From the day a puppy is born it has an instinctive drive not only to survive but eventually to become a pack member, and one of its tools is the ability to get attention. Dogs that demand your attention on cue, by order, by stealth, or by looking dolefully into your eyes, get noticed. Dogs that get noticed get on in life, and that is why dogs seek our attention.

So what's wrong with a bit of attention seeking? Well, the main problem is that when we want our dogs' attention it should be on our terms, not theirs. Most dogs, if allowed to do so, think that it is a better deal when they grab our attention for their use and ultimately command our time and lifestyle. Passive dominance it may be, but dogs love to be control freaks!

The subtext to this behavior is "Why will you not pay me any attention?"

Anyone who has had the experience of bringing up children will know a great deal about sibling rivalry and attention-grabbing behavior. This habit is pretty well developed in humans as well as dogs. Dogs are even better at demanding attention than most children. If they were not, people like me would not have a job.

Left: Some dogs use barking as a tactic to demand attention from their owners. And a very effective tactic it can be, as continual barking is very irritating and is virtually guaranteed to provoke a reaction.

Below: Dominant dogs like to grab their owner's attention. Pats and strokes are indicators that the dog is viewed as a high-ranking member of the pack, and he may behave aggressively to other dogs in the house to reinforce his status.

The other dog in the household is looking downcast because she is not getting stroked.

Attention Trip

Excessive attention seeking on your dog's terms simply means that the behavior is so overdeveloped that it is unbearable. You cannot go about your daily chores without tripping over the dog, which has already worked out yet another way of interrupting your routine, like sitting on your knee—all 100 pounds of him. Attention he definitely gets, and of course, it is to his benefit.

Of course, the point at which attention seeking becomes a nuisance rather than a pleasure depends on your character as well as the dog's. Some people simply love and encourage their dog's attention as it makes them feel needed and loved. In this case, it actually adds to their well-being—and to their dog's likewise. However,

*Left: A German Shepherd on your lap is just what you do **not** want when you settle down on a chair for a rest. The best response here would be to stand up immediately while avoiding eye contact and the temptation to shout at the dog.*

Above: When you can't even sit down without the dog hopping onto the chair ahead of you for attention, he has gained the upper hand. It is time for remedial action.

in other cases, the dog's attention seeking has a negative effect, disrupting the owner's lifestyle, and at that point the dog/human relationship is on the rocks.

The majority of dogs presented to me for excessive attention seeking are in fact the toy breeds like Yorkies or Pekingese. Their small size makes it very tempting to pick them up and cuddle them all the time, with the result that they become overattached and never learn to stand on their own feet. Problems are also common with insecure rescue dogs. Here the temptation is to compensate for their poor start in life by lavishing attention on them—only to find that the more you give, the more the dog demands.

Tackling the Problem

So what's going on? Dominance is what's going on, or, to be more specific, passive dominance—a helplessness that demands attention from owners and friends.

These dogs basically want to become top dog in the attention department. The rules of the pack are simple: use your brain to get what you want and when you want it. The only way this can be stopped is by a smarter, more consistent fellow pack member—i.e.,

you—acting like a higher-ranking and more dominant dog. If you have problems with your dog's behavior, then you have to act like the boss all of the time.

The end result will be your dog changing into a well-behaved companion—and moreover a dog that loves and respects you even more because you are an excellent pack leader. Strong leaders lead: they do not fawn over the pack members.

Some people don't like dogs, and the feeling is mutual. They don't pay any attention to the dog, and as a consequence the dog ignores them. Those of us who do like dogs can learn from such people what turns dogs off—and use it to our advantage.

Below: Attention addicts, whether dominant or insecure, need or want attention on demand. If you give in, the dog will expect to gets his way every time until the habit becomes embedded.

Left: Toy breeds in particular can develop attention seeking to an undesirable degree because they become used to being picked up and generally pampered by their doting owners.

Dogs can be manipulative—rolling over for a pat is a good way of securing someone's attention.

What Is Excessive?

While there's little doubt that this behavior problem is learned, there is a lot of difference of opinion as to what is excessive. What one owner thinks is much too much may be quite acceptable to another. Inconsistencies can also occur within families, causing variations in reaction that simply confuse a dog and make it more difficult to alter the behavior.

This happens when some visitors encourage your dog's advances with rewards (touch, praise, rough play) while other visitors lose their cool at the sight of a single dog hair on their clothes. The dog is still being intermittently rewarded, so will continue to try to solicit more attention until all visitors ignore his advances—and continue to do so until the behavior ceases to be a problem. This may even mean your leading the dog into the house on a collar and lead and popping the end of the lead over a hook or fixture to keep him at bay until he has calmed down after visitors have arrived (see the hook restriction program in Chapter 3).

Of course, most dogs work by stealth—especially when you are on your own. Many owners fall into the trap of petting their dog whenever he seeks attention. When they think they have shown him enough attention, they stop and expect the dog to understand that they have been

Left: As with so many of the behavioral problems described in this book, inconsistency makes it harder to correct a problem. If some visitors are happy to pet an attention-seeking dog like this while others ignore it, the dog will continue to solicit attention because she knows that she stands a chance of being rewarded with a pat.

fair. He doesn't. All he knows is that he can demand attention with a fair degree of success. So pat your dog only when petting is initiated by you. At all other times, ignore him.

Many crafty dogs bring toys for you to throw—and yes, we, being humans,

Right: If you have real problems with a dog that pesters anyone that comes to visit you, it pays to put the dog on a lead and drop the end of the lead over a hook in another room. The dog should be allowed to greet visitors only once she has calmed down.

are pleased, impressed, or made to feel important by such cleverness. Don't be deceived. This is indeed clever, but it is just another ploy which the dog has learned to control you and get attention. Don't respond at all. Keep your hands still and your mouth shut, and wait until your dog becomes bored and goes away. Then maybe later, get the toy, throw it, make him bring it and release it. When the game is over, put the toy away. Again your dog will see you behaving like the boss and respect you for it. In time he can still have fun on your (not his) terms, and eventually his pestering tactics will cease.

Below 1 and 2: *This is another clever way of gaining attention— the dog heads off and reappears with a favorite toy in his mouth that he wants you to throw for him to retrieve. It may seem like innocent fun, but the dog is trying to control the agenda; ignore his demands.*

①

②

Eventually the dog will get bored and give up the game.

Below right: *It's at times like these that you do not need a dog pestering for attention. The mother wants to spend time playing with her tiny baby and does not want to have to use her other hand to fend off the attentions of the dog.*

While showing affection for the baby, the mother should give the dog some food treats in a rubber food toy. This will serve as a pleasant distraction.

Left: *Learn to harden your heart and turn your back on a dog that is pestering you. By ignoring the dog, he will come to realize that the behavior carries no rewards.*

How to Prevent Attention Seeking

Teach your dog that it's normal for him to spend time on his own again—see some of the tips on tackling separation anxiety in Chapter 5. Build up gradually from five minutes to one hour twice daily, over several weeks. Whenever your dog nudges you or looks at you with doleful eyes, ignore him completely. Even if he starts crawling over you, which is unlikely, don't push him off as the mere physical touch can be construed by the dog as a reward.

Moreover remember that to **ignore** the dog is your best training device. In the short term, if a dog is impossible and you find it very difficult to ignore him, then using some deterrent spray on your person or your seating area will deter him from coming near you. Orange or lemon peel rubbed on

But the dog enjoys the fact of being touched.

Preoccupied on the phone, the woman pushes the dog away.

The nudging and pawing are all meant to say, "Why don't you talk to me?"

Above 1, 2, and 3: Dogs that crave attention often use pestering tactics like this to gain your attention when you are otherwise occupied. Pushing the dog away isn't a good way of rebuffing his approaches. The dog may interpret your touch as a reward.

your hands may discourage the endless nudging with which some dogs seek attention. Large powerful dogs that literally throw themselves at you may need a set of training disks (see Chapter 2) to dissuade them from bullying you into giving them attention—but don't use these on very sensitive dogs or young puppies.

Points to Remember

- Make sure that any attention is on your terms: you decide when enough is enough. So always ignore your dog if he requests attention.
- Make all the family and any visitors follow the same rules. Consistency is important.
- Remember that as far as a dog is concerned, being pushed off could be construed as a reward. To a dog,

> ### ▶ Taking Control—Recap
>
> - ▶ **Ignore attention-seeking approaches—the message is "Don't tell me when to stroke you."**
> - ▶ **Use deterrent spray on your chair—"Don't approach my seat."**
> - ▶ **Rub orange or lemon peel on your hands—"Don't nudge me."**
> - ▶ **Use training disks or a deterrent spray—under expert guidance.**
> - ▶ **Remember that friends and family must treat the dog in the same way. Consistency is important.**

touch is very potent praise—so what you intend as discouragement can be interpreted by him as encouragement to continue!

- If your dog tries to get on your lap, simply stand up quickly and allow him to slip off before he gets comfortable. No eye contact, no shouting. Bob up and down like a yo-yo if necessary until you get peace.
- Obedience train your dog to get down and stay, then use this when the dog is being demanding. Teach the dog to go and stay in his bed as a fun game—use a reward. When the dog has got the message in a positive way (usually after ten or more

lessons), then this can also be used to get some relief.

I have found that most dogs respond well to the above treatment. If you remember how your dog learned to get attention in the first place, you will now know what not to do. Eventually, you can reinstate a moderate amount of affectionate response on your terms and may be able to relax most of the procedures. However, a few dogs are so conditioned to effusive and frequent response from their owners that praise and affection always have to be kept to a minimum. Otherwise, the dog's attention seeking begins to increase once again and becomes intolerable.

A gentle stroke rewards the dog for behaving as you want her to do.

Left 1, 2, and 3: Obedience training is really helpful in dealing with a determined attention seeker. Once your dog has got used to the idea of being sent to his bed from time to time—a tidbit reward helps to imprint this behavior—you can command the dog to go and stay there when you want a bit of peace and quiet.

▶Destructive Behavior

Why Are Dogs Destructive?

Coming in to find your dog munching on your favorite slippers is not everyone's idea of the ideal owner-dog relationship. Of course, from the dog's point of view, there's nothing wrong with chewing tasty leather or soft

material—it's only natural to investigate objects by smell and taste, and anyway it's great fun. We can accept that, but it's only natural for us to become upset when our dog chews something that we value. We need to remember that dogs don't share our sense of values. For your dog, there's no difference between an old slipper and a new one or between a soft toy and the fringes of an expensive rug.

Most destructive behavior is caused by one of three factors:

▶ **Normal puppy behavior.** It's natural for a puppy to investigate the exciting new world, often by chewing as much of it as possible.

▶ **Boredom.** When a dog is insufficiently active or stimulated, as it grows from puppy to adult dog, it specifically targets certain items in the house to play with (in its view) or damage (our view).

▶ **Separation anxiety.** This is the commonest reason for destructive activity. A dog that has not learned to be alone becomes stressed when left, and may seek relief in frantic action, often trying to dig or chew through doors and windows. This behavior may be accompanied by urination, defecation, barking, and whining. If you believe this is your dog's problem, see Chapter 5 for the way to tackle separation anxiety.

Right: If you come home to a scene like this, it's too late to punish the dog. He will not associate your displeasure with his earlier act of chewing the cushion.

Prevention is the best remedy, and even though many people coping with this problem will have adult dogs in whom the behavior is already well ingrained, it's worth starting by looking at prevention.

Prevention Advice
(for puppies and newly acquired dogs)

It is important to have a dog who can be left unsupervised. So from an early age, gradually accustom your dog to being left alone; aim to work up to periods of one hour. Don't encourage him to be under your feet all day. Instead, allow him to spend time by himself in the yard, on the patio, in a dog pen or another room while you're elsewhere. This encourages self-reliance and prevents a dog from becoming overly dependent upon its owner—this is especially important in a one person–one dog relationship.

A new dog or puppy should never be allowed to roam the house freely for the first few months until you are able to judge its all-round behavior. Most chewing takes place in your absence, so by curtailing your dog's freedom, you limit any damage to a single location, which is easier to deal with. Moreover, in the kitchen, for instance, you can implement preventative actions to teach the dog what he can and cannot chew. Eventually, you can open up the house to the dog if that's your desire.

Above 1–3: This sort of destructive behavior can be a sign of boredom.

Exercise and Food

Exercising your dog before you leave him can help to burn off pent-up energy. He will be more likely to curl up and go to sleep than to rampage through the house. Tired dogs chew less!

Consider feeding your dog before you leave the house (but make sure he's had ample time to evacuate his bowels before you go out). Satiated dogs become sleepy and lethargic, and are less inclined to chew.

Cage Training

Puppies should become accustomed to an indoor cage from day one. Ensure that your dog sees the cage as a refuge rather than a prison by providing marrow bones, toys stuffed with treats, or chew bones to keep him occupied in it while you're out. But when you return, make sure you collect the chews and keep them for next time you go out; otherwise your dog will not find them interesting. Feeding the dog in the cage once or twice daily also helps to condition him to accept it as a positive amenity.

If the destruction takes place in your absence, then it may be for the reasons mentioned above. Dogs that have not become gradually accustomed to your absence may become anxious when left. These dogs are the ones that follow you about the house or seek contact with you whatever you're doing. They must be taught that being alone is not the end of the world.

Recap

▶ **Accustom your dog to spending time away from the family.**

▶ **Restrict access to rooms within the home until your dog has learned how to behave.**

  ▶ **Don't leave him alone and full of energy—tire him out first.**

    ▶ **Feeding him before you go out will leave him more inclined to have a postdinner nap than for activity.**

      ▶ **Consider using an indoor cage—but make it attractive to the dog and large enough for him.**

Direct Action

Punishing destructive behavior can be difficult because we're often not at home when the destruction takes place. Punishment after the event is useless. If you come in and find your house trashed with the perpetrator peacefully asleep among the wreckage, it's only natural to feel angry with him. But it doesn't come naturally to him to link your immediate anger with something he did earlier. All punishment will achieve is to confuse him. All you can usefully do at this stage is to clear up and resolve to begin a retraining program immediately. However, if your dog is destructive in your presence or you catch him in the act, then there are a couple of measures you can use.

Above 1, 2, and 3: Frequently this sort of destructive behavior will take place when you are out of the house— a hapless toy bears the brunt of the animal's feelings of frustration and anxiety at being left on her own.

Have several ready-filled water pistols about the house. When you catch your dog chewing, squirt water at his head, simultaneously commanding "No." (Alternatively, you can simply use the squirt without the command.) As the dog comes to associate chewing with an unpleasant squirt, he is less likely to fancy this activity. However, this approach is effective with puppies and dogs in the early stages of destructive chewing only and will not affect dogs exhibiting anxiety-related destructive behavior.

Left: "Who, me?" Try not to give way to your anger and punish a dog when you come home and find a trail of damage around the house. The dog will be pleased to see you and will not associate a rebuke with her earlier actions. Harsh words at this time will only confuse the animal that expects a greeting from you.

A more direct means of training by association is to throw a bunch of training disks, or car keys near the dog' legs when you catch him chewing so that the noise distracts him and interrupts his actions. Most dogs realize you are the thrower, so don't bother trying to disguise the fact. (See also Chapter 2 on how to use training disks.) When using the water pistol or training disks, remember that it's vital that all correction takes place at the time of the incident.

Deterrent Measures—Recap

▶ **Keep a water pistol or training disks handy for when you catch your dog in the act. And all dogs should learn the command "No."**

▶ **Don't punish by hitting or shouting at the dog.**

▶ **Don't punish a dog after the event.**

Below left: If you actually catch your dog in the act of chewing, then you can use deterrent measures such as a squirt of water or the clatter or training disks employed in conjunction with the command "No."

Don't expect instant results with a destructive dog— you will need patience.

Above: Use a firm tone of voice to reprimand a dog that has misbehaved, but don't resort to shouts or smacks. It is counterproductive.

Do not physically hit the dog, take hold of him, or shout at him, as this is less effective. In some cases, it even encourages the dog to chew, for it may interpret this as a reward—after all, for some clever dogs attention of any kind is better than none.

Bitter Experience

If you have a dog that primarily chews specific objects, say the kitchen furniture or a particular item of footwear, first try and use a deterrent spray. In this way, the dog learns from her own actions that chewing these things is an unpleasant experience that leads to a bitter taste in her mouth.

When I have a new dog, I spend the first two weeks spraying the knobs on the kitchen furniture with deterrent spray daily, sometimes twice a day. This means that on every occasion that the dog attempts to chew, she experiences an unpleasant taste. Dogs don't repeat unpleasant experiences too often. Repetitive bitter experiences put the dog off the knobs. The weakness in this procedure is often the owners. They forget to keep up the spraying or think that an occasional squirt is enough. It isn't—you need to fix it in the dog's mind that these items always taste bad. It is wise to spray the objects when your dog is not in the room and leave a window open for ten minutes before allowing the dog back in. This ensures that the dog can distinguish the spray scent on the objects to be avoided rather than sensing its presence throughout the room.

Above: Items of furniture, electrical wiring, slippers and shoes, baskets, even oven gloves can appear on the menu of a dog that is determined to ease its anxiety by chewing something.

Simultaneously, leave the dog a chew and interesting toys—the kind designed to be stuffed with food that the dog can extract a bit at a time is ideal. This means that while the deterrent spray steers him away from forbidden objects, he has something that is permissible and pleasant to chew.

When dealing with puppies at the chewing stage, I spray all electrical wires, plugs, and sockets daily to deter the puppy from even considering them as chewable. Ideally with puppies, all wires should be out of reach or left unplugged. The same technique can be used on other items that your dog chews.

Below 1, 2, and 3: Sometimes destructive behavior around the kitchen will also involve scavenging for food from a trash bin. In such cases, regular applications of a deterrent spray can put the dog off nosing around the target bin.

❶   ❷   ❸

Useful Tips

▶ Dogs are intelligent creatures—keep their minds occupied with fun games.

▶ Don't tell a dog off after you have discovered damage. It has no effect except to teach the animal that you are oddly unpredictable.

▶ If damage is intolerable, use an appropriately sized cage—but only for short periods not exceeding two hours.

▶ If a particular deterrent spray doesn't work, look around for different types. Something should be effective.

▶ Secure or lock away all bins and trash cans.

Left: Remember to spray vulnerable objects, like leather shoes, on a regular basis. It is no good forgetting about the plan after only a day or two of remedial action.

Right: In very obstinate cases, you may have to consider keeping the dog in a kennel and pen outside the house for a while.

Below: Another useful tactic when dealing with a destructive or scavenging dog like this is to leave a chew or food-filled toy as a distraction; the dog finds it is more fun to chew the treat than the furniture.

If in severe cases your dog's behavior is resistant to discouragement, then you may need to consider using an outside pen and kennel for a few months until the problem can be dealt with properly. Your dog will need to be gradually accustomed to using the pen, working up from five minutes two to three times daily. Remember to leave him some interesting toys filled with treats. Then when you're not at home, you can leave your dog knowing he is quite safe—and so is your home.

▶ Play Biting

Most dog owners have experienced that little nip on one or more of their fingers as they try to play with the new puppy member of the family. Because the new puppy arrives with the most adorable expression of innocence, the exuberance and accompanying mouthing are often forgiven. Yes, puppies appear to have been designed to bring the most stoical and resolute person to their emotional knees despite the pain of a bitten finger.

Hard play-bites may provoke aggression.

quickly learn how hard they can bite without upsetting a playmate. If they bite too hard, then the other puppy will respond by becoming aggressive or will cease playing. Puppies instinctively wish to dominate their littermates, and biting is also a part of their dominance armory. The puppies learn how and when to use their teeth with their littermates, one

Left and below: Rough-and-tumble games and tug-of-war contests over a prized toy are all part of the way in which one dog seeks to assert his dominance over a fellow pack member. Puppies practice play biting in the same way.

Puppies develop sharp needlelike teeth that appear to be rather excessive for such small creatures. Though the teeth are for eating food, another use is to help other littermates learn bite inhibition and how much pressure to use on one another. Sharp puppy teeth hurt without causing real damage. So when a litter of puppies are play fighting, they

useful set of social rules for future canine relationships. They also use games of strength to assert their pack positions. Wolves, pups, and domestic dogs use body slamming to dominate or test the strength of the opposition. Children learn a similar set of rules: overaggressive children are avoided by the others, so moderation promotes inclusion.

Why Dogs Play Bite Us

When puppies leave the litter and arrive in our homes, they bring with them their experiences, one of which is using their mouth—play biting, mouthing, nibbling, and play growling. Investigative mouthing behavior is exhibited at a very young age in puppies for a number of different reasons. But when humans take the place of littermates, puppies can become confused.

Play biting by puppies must not be encouraged.

Without correct training, continued mouthing can develop into habitual play biting. Though it is termed "play," what we are really talking about is dogs and puppies actually biting people, which hurts!

A common scenario occurs when a puppy wishes to initiate play or attention. The puppy nips the owner who reacts, either by pushing the puppy away—which he interprets as joining in the game—or by encouraging rough play games. Either way, the puppy learns that play biting is acceptable. Early dominance behavior like growling or snapping can also be a problem,

Left: Puppies are so cute that we tend to forgive them when they give us a nip during playtime.

Here the mouth is used to express affection.

Right: Unless corrected, puppies that mouth people can turn into habitual play biters.

though this is less common in very young puppies. But whatever is happening, it should be discouraged and stopped swiftly.

In the same way that primates use their hands, dogs use their mouths for innumerable purposes, including affection, touching, and testing, which are expressions of play. If we watch dogs at play, we see a great deal of play biting and mouthing, especially around the neck area, as rough-and-tumble games ensue. Dog trainers and breeders who watch their dogs interacting will have seen many times that sudden aggressive outburst in a game between two dogs, when one of the dogs bites too hard and the recipient yelps or becomes angry and bites back, generally bringing the game to a close. The bitten dog no longer wants to play and is now ignoring his friend. If play is to continue, the biter will have to learn to use his teeth more gently.

Above: Dogs use their mouths for more than just eating and barking. Their mouths are part of the sensory equipment with which they investigate the world around them, other animals, and their owners.

Dogs have their own natural response mechanisms to various interactions with fellow canines and innate skills like pressure sensitivity, speed, and timing. We don't. Therefore, it is not a good idea to begin imitating dog behavior. Instead, we can use our understanding of canine psychology to deter play biting—a more subtle approach than biting back!

Play Biting Is Painful

I know many dogs that play bite gently or take their owner's hand into their mouths. Their owners don't find this a problem, and the behavior has not worsened. Personally, I believe that no dog should be allowed such familiarity if it is to be a safe companion—especially with children. Moreover, if you have young children, even gentle play biting or mouthing can be frightening to them. It can also lead to more serious rough behavior, including later dominance aggression. If it is never allowed to develop, there is little likelihood of it getting out of hand. You must make the choice.

Most people genuinely don't like being bitten, in fun or otherwise. Our reactions are often sufficient to teach the puppy that we do not like what they are doing, and the game is over. Unfortunately, when nipped, we naturally recoil. Children especially react in a defensive manner, which encourages the puppy (or dog). Instead of learning not to bite, she learns to bite more. As time goes on, the puppy can become even more dominant and she finds this behavior rewarding. She bites, you pull your hand or clothing away, and then a tug-of-war ensues, which is even more fun.

A typical scenario goes like this. The puppy grabs a trouser leg; the owner hears the little growls from this tiny pup and thinks it is charming. The owner moves his leg and makes a little game of it—the puppy responds to the preylike movements and really starts to enjoy the game. Many weeks and games later, when the puppy

Above: Children love romping with a dog, but don't allow play biting to be part of the game. It may frighten the child and lead to worse aggression or very rough play.

Right: It may seem fun when a puppy nips and tugs at your trouser leg in play, but if you let the behavior go unchecked, the situation can deteriorate. The puppy gets bigger and the habit harder to stop.

is now four times the size and weight, it gets out of hand and the owner responds with shouting, slapping, and eventually, when this no longer works, shutting the dog in another room.

The pup or adolescent dog has learned that she is dominant and that she normally wins the game, and that's

Right: Only play tug-of-war games with your dog if he observes the ground rules—ultimately you must always win the game.

If the dog starts to react aggressively, it's game over.

The dog must release the toy when he is told to.

what being a dog is all about. As the dog gets rougher, the owner's shouting and aggression increase—all very rewarding in terms of canine play. By this stage, of course, young children are hopelessly unable to deal with the dog and also begin to avoid her rough play biting. Unfortunately, the dog has now been conditioned to play bite. Shutting the dog in another room only makes her frustrated, hyperactive, and keener than ever to enjoy her dominant play-time. The next stage is that the dog is brought to my center for retraining.

Toy or Prey

Many toys on the market are designed for human/dog fun, for example tough fabric ropes made for tug-of-war games. They are safe when used with a strict set of rules—notably that the owner always wins and that the dog allows you, on command, to take the toy away at any time without a fight or any grumbling. Thousands of dogs enjoy the exercise and the mind-stimulating game, and so do their owners. However, it is inadvisable to allow children under the age of 12 to play tug-of-war with dogs unless

supervised and important to insist that they play by the rules above.

If you notice the dog beginning to growl and becoming overstimulated and aggressive, take that as your signal to end that type of tug-of-war game; maybe for good. Also see Chapter 3 on handling a dominant dog. Many of the terrier and guarding breeds also need to be monitored, as they tend to inherit dominant characteristics. The terrier likes shaking toys as he would a rat, and the tug-of-war rope is an outlet for that natural behavior. It's perfectly harmless so long as it isn't your finger that's involved.

When I was a dog handler in the Police Dog Section, we taught dogs to attack criminals and bite them. The basic training tool was the retrieve, combined with tug-of-war games using stuffed and rope-type toys. Now if that is the best way to teach police dogs to bite criminals, then it's pretty clear what games we should allow pet dogs to play or not to play and under what rules.

Above: The way this terrier is shaking the toy reminds us that dogs like this are hunters by nature—this is how he kills rats.

The Evil Eye

This advice will apply mostly to puppies but is also worth using with any newly acquired adult dog. From day one, avoid playing any games that involve mouthing, i.e., teeth on skin. If your puppy tries to solicit attention from you by play biting, ignore him. Just get up and walk away. Alternatively, take hold of the puppy by the scruff and say "No" firmly, looking directly into his eyes for about two seconds. The command must be delivered sharply and crisply. Then let the dog go and ignore him. This is normally enough to discourage play biting in the very early stages, say between six and 18 weeks, and it teaches your puppy the useful "No" command.

If the puppy or adolescent dog has already developed play biting to a high degree and resistance to his owner's countermeasures is severe, then hold-

Right: Play biting can be a problem with dogs, whatever their size.

Below: Use the firm command "No" and then ignore a dog that pesters you and tries play biting to gain your attention. If the dog persists, get up and walk away.

ing the scruff may be seen by the dog as more rough play or a dominant threat, so it is best just to say "No" and then ignore him.

With an adult dog, leaving a lead trailing behind him—only when you are present—is also an excellent method to stop determined play biters. By grabbing the lead you automatically get instant control—you can drop the lead end onto a wall hook, and instantly the dog is prevented from continuing his play biting

Left: Don't allow any games that involve play biting—this is especially important with a small baby in the house.

If you don't have a hook on the baseboard, the valve of a radiator works just as well.

1 **2** **3**

Left and above 1, 2, and 3: If you are having to cope with an adult dog that habitually play bites, it is a good idea to attach a lead to the animal when you are in the house. Then, if the dog starts to play bite, you can pick up the lead to gain control and drop the end of the lead over a hook.

when you move out of his reach. Alternatively, with large dogs (not puppies), you can check the dog with the lead, giving maybe four or five checks within as many seconds. The point is not to hurt the dog's neck but to interrupt the undesirable action. I call this the Rapid Check. It is uncomfortable for the dog, it is quick, and the play biting is no longer fun. If the dog begins again, I simply repeat the Rapid Check but always accompanied with the command "No." I will then drop the lead and continue with whatever I was doing. If the dog begins again, I repeat the Rapid Check.

By using the lead and collar, you are not touching the dog's body, which reduces any contact that the dog might

Understand the Situation

▶ **It is natural for dogs to use their mouths as a tool to help them explore the world around them. We need to learn how to discourage or redirect that behavior when it is inappropriate in a domestic setting.**

Right: A soft toy can be a useful distraction—the puppy learns to have fun with the toy rather than play biting.

take as rough play or reward. Never hit out with your hand or have a screaming match with your dog. Dogs are faster than we are and therefore simply enjoy the game of "I play bite, you hit out and miss, I dive in again." They have even more fun—on the dogs' terms, not ours.

Dog Training

The traditional (and still the best) way to prevent or stop play biting is to obedience train your dog. Puppies should be trained from six weeks onward. Learn from a video or get a trainer to teach you early puppy training in your own home. Concentrate on the "Down, stay" position. When this has been mastered, you can command your dog to do this when he tries to play bite. If your dog play bites, do what his littermates would do: give a puppy yelp ("Ouch!") and refuse to play momentarily. You will eventually enjoy your dog's company more—and he will love you even more for making the rules clear.

Redirecting the Play

Throwing a toy or a ball is another distraction method that I use—especially in the park and garden but in the home as well. Squeaky toys are ideal. Directing the dog's attention to a toy instead of your hand is a very safe and effective way of reducing play biting and at the same time teaching the dog what he can use his teeth on.

Some dogs mouth their owner's hand when being walked. If your dog grabs your hand while you are holding the lead, snap the lead sharply, ignore the dog, and carry on walking as if nothing has happened. Don't give the dog any attention at all. If you react like this consistently, your dog will find mouthing your hand not much fun. You can also try using a deterrent spray. Spray your hand and the lead just before embarking on the walk. Taste deterrents work on most dogs, especially if used for many weeks to ensure that the lesson is well implanted.

Below 1: One of the most effective ways of stopping a play biter from persisting with the habit is to obedience train her to a high standard from an early age.

Below 2: This dog is being taught the "Down, stay" command. Once a dog has been conditioned to behave correctly when she hears the command, you have a powerful tool at your disposal to interrupt unwanted behavior and gain control over the animal.

Left: Dogs do not like the experience of mouthing something that has been treated with a bitter-tasting spray. If your dog mouths your hand while on a walk, spray your hand and the lead before you set off.

In the home, your dog may be an armchair mouther, constantly reaching for your hand when you are sitting down. Again, a deterrent spray applied to your hand each time you settle down will discourage this behavior.

Below 3: A tidbit is given when the dog has obeyed the command as a reward to reinforce the desired behavior.

▶ Redirection—Recap

- ▶ **Don't reward mouthing by responding—ignore it.**
- ▶ **Distract a play biter with a favorite toy.**
- ▶ **Use deterrent spray to make mouthing an unpleasant experience.**

Above: It is great when a family and their pet develop a close bond, but it must be on the right terms—the dog must respect her owners and not be indulged when she shows signs of wanting to play bite humans.

▶ Useful Tips

- ▶ **Deterrent sprays on vulnerable areas—clothing or children's arms— make mouthing a distasteful experience. Do check that the deterrent used is harmless to dogs—and children.**
- ▶ **Consider using training disks with dogs that have been conditioned to their use (see Chapter 2).**
- ▶ **Ignore undesirable approaches from the dog—don't respond to them.**

▶ Jumping Up

Dogs seem to be obsessed with face-to-face contact, wanting to lick and nudge our faces and mouths with theirs. Between dogs this is an important social action, serving as a greeting, a plea for an adult dog to regurgitate food, and even a sign of submission. When it's directed at a human, the height difference means that they learn to jump up to reach our faces. As we're not dogs, face licking is a habit we don't normally like. The associated jumping up is even more of a nuisance. It can also be dangerous, especially when big dogs and small children or elderly people are involved.

Like most habits, this one starts in puppyhood. Puppies are small, so we naturally bend down or lift them up, giving them the perfect opportunity to lick our faces. As the puppy grows, it's natural for him to try to continue the behavior by jumping toward faces.

Above: Puppies and young dogs love it when they can lick our faces and thrust their noses toward our mouths. This may be an inheritance from wolf behavior where pack members solicit in this way for morsels of regurgitated food as a treat.

Prevention Advice

While following this advice, it's important that everyone the dog jumps upon partakes in any retraining program. Everyone must use identical commands and actions, or the dog will become confused and even less responsive. No half measures please! Young children should always learn in the company of a capable adult.

Four Paws on the Ground

If you have a puppy, don't allow him to lick faces, especially where children are involved. Hygiene is one factor, but also it's dangerous—a grown dog can easily knock someone over. When you greet your dog, command "Sit," and offer praise only when your puppy has all four paws on the ground. If he does jump up, stand absolutely still and say nothing. To the puppy this is boring, and he'll quickly learn that there's no fun or reward to be had by jump-ing up. All the family and any visitors must participate in this program consistently if the behavior is to be stopped.

When your dog jumps up on people indiscriminately in parks and in the street, this can be more

Sharp claws can inflict painful scratches as the dog scrambles for attention.

Left: When we are not down at their level, dogs that are prone to jumping up bridge the height difference by getting up on their hind legs. With big, strong dogs behavior like this can be quite a problem—it's easy to be caught off balance.

difficult to control. It's often difficult to stop dog lovers from petting your dog when he jumps up on them—but only in this way can you hope to prevent this behavior. Many people, especially children, find puppies irresistible, and here a retractable lead can be useful to control a puppy's exploration of a new world full of people who love puppies and unwittingly love teaching them just what you don't want—to jump up.

▶ Prevention Advice—Recap

▶ **Don't respond to jumping up by shouting, smacking, or pushing away—step back, turn away, and ignore.**

▶ **Ignore a jumping puppy: praise a puppy only when all four feet are on the ground.**

▶ **Use a retractable lead in the park to control jumping at passing dog lovers.**

Retraining your dog will require patience and a calm disposition.

Right: Four paws are on the ground—good! The dog can have a treat as a reward.

Owners often try to deter their dog by hitting him or pushing him off, to no avail. Unfortunately, for most dogs, any kind of touch is a strong reward, so they can interpret what is intended as a corrective measure as encouragement—a rough kind of game. Over time, the dog's resistance to his owner's efforts builds up, wearing the owner down and toughening up the dog.

Left and below 1 and 2: When training a dog to stop jumping, all the family must adopt the same commands. Adults may have to monitor children.

1

2

Initial Triggers That Teach Dogs to Jump Up

When we are sitting down and a little pup jumps up, placing her front paws on our knees, it's a natural response to lean forward (trigger 1) and either stroke the puppy (trigger 2) or, even worse, lift her onto our lap for a cuddle (trigger 3). Three reinforcements have taken place, laying the foundations for a dog that jumps up in the future. Even if you then put the dog back on the floor, she has learned an important association: jumping up brings rewards. Dogs that are lifted onto a lap obviously enjoy the contact, but it's unfair to do this with a puppy and expect her to understand when she is bigger that you no longer want her on your knees. It's even more confusing to her if you let her jump on you but not on your friends. Dogs need black-and-white rules, not complex "sometimes do, sometimes don't" situations. Teach what you want for the long term, not for the immediate moment.

It may be wiser to play with the puppy on the floor. Such play is far more interactive and coincidentally removes the pup's need or wish to jump up. Of course, many readers will have dogs who are already expert at jumping up and getting their own way. Whether the motivation is dominance, demanding attention, or seeking affection, let's look at some methods to counter the dog's expertise.

I'm Home, I'm Ignoring You

Aim to eliminate whatever excites the jumping up. For example, if your dog jumps up when you return home, then stop greeting her when you come in. At each homecoming ignore her for the first 15 minutes. Keep your hands still, and don't even say hello. Ensure that all family members do the same. At first it will be difficult. Because your dog is used to an effusive greeting, she will probably be somewhat confused at first. However, as the reward of being pushed off, stroked, or praised is no longer forthcoming, the reason for jumping will have gone. Your dog should soon learn that there's no point in continuing to jump up. After the first 15 minutes,

1

2

Below 1, 2, and 3: If your dog jumps up when you are sitting in a chair, avoid giving him any pats or strokes and simply stand up, forcing him to drop onto all fours again. Ignore him until he stops acting in this way.

3

your own efforts, then you'll have a dog that listens to your commands.

If your dog learns to sit on command then, whenever she's about to jump up, instruct "Sit." When she sits, praise her verbally. Make sure that jumping up is always ignored, never rewarded. Once she realizes that, she'll prefer to sit for greetings.

Above: Children naturally play with a puppy on the floor, and we can all learn from that. If you also get down on the ground to play games with a puppy, he will not feel the urge to jump at you to gain your attention.

you can call her to you, tell her to sit, and give a reward that does not overexcite her. You have now simply reorganized the time and manner of greeting to suit you. Dogs adapt with no hard feelings.

The Ignore exercise is also useful around the home when your dog suddenly jumps up at you. As soon as she jumps up, pivot away from her, with no eye contact and no commands. When she gets the message, tell her to sit, praise her, and maybe offer a small treat. Ignore her again if she becomes excitable. The dog will learn that her action does not get the reaction she wants but that staying calm and quiet is rewarded with the desired attention.

Dog Training

Obedience training, combined with the Ignore exercise described above all, has the highest chance of success. If you train your dog to a high standard, through a reputable club or through

Above 1 and 2: Praise the dog when he responds obediently to your command to "Sit." You must reward only correct behavior.

Left: It looks like the cold shoulder, but it does pay dividends to ignore a dog that jumps up at you in a frenzy when you return home. The dog will start to learn that jumping brings no rewards.

Redirect Unwanted Greetings

If your dog loves retrieving games with toys or balls, then take one with you to the park. For the first ten lessons, make sure the dog does not have access to any of his retrieve toys at home. As soon as you see your dog about to pay unwanted attention to a passerby, call him and throw his ball or toy. This is a good distraction method for dogs that like retrieving. Timing is vital, so attract your dog's attention before he jumps on someone, not afterward. Using a whistle to signify a game helps to get the dog's attention before you throw the toy.

If your dog is difficult to control, tell him to sit when he brings the ball back and at once connect his lead. Then briskly walk off away from his target person. Show him the ball as you go, exciting him a little. After about 50 yards (45 m), unclip his lead and throw the ball again for him to retrieve. This also teaches the dog that having the lead clipped on him does not necessarily mean the end of his walk. He cannot predict your actions, therefore you stay in charge.

Water and Sound Deterrents

(for determined and dominant dogs only)
This method is best suited to dogs that have long-established jumping up problems, very big dogs that can hurt people by jumping up, and dogs that need to be retrained quickly because children or old people are involved. You will need a water pistol or a dog repellent sound alarm. To back up this method, it is important to deal with the root cause of the

Above: Special collars that emit a sound alarm can be used to stop a dog that wants to jump up.

Right 2: Praise your dog when he brings the toy back to you. This tactic redirects the dog's attention away from the passerby and onto the toy instead.

Right 1: If you have difficulty when out for a walk in the park because your dog tends to jump up at passing strangers, try taking a ball or favorite toy with you. When the dog is about to jump up at someone, throw the toy and encourage the dog to chase after and retrieve it.

1

2

Right: A water pistol or plant spray is an effective deterrent measure that will take even large, pushy dogs by surprise. When the dog makes you the victim of its unwanted attention, a quick squirt of water accompanied by the command "No" should cause him to get down quickly.

unpleasant squirt of water, and this will discourage his bad habit. Again it's important for all family members to take part if your dog is to learn. Some dogs find a sound alarm more offputting than a water pistol.

Smell and Taste Deterrents

(for determined and dominant dogs only)

Bitter apple and other safe, nontoxic dog repellent scents are also useful to dissuade dogs from jumping upon us. This I find especially helpful with children or the elderly. Of course, children also need training not to confuse the dog and not to teach him to jump up in the first place. It's often hard for a child to understand why some canine actions are undesirable, and patience is needed all around.

If the dog jumps up on the child when you are nearby, spray the air about the dog (or the child can do this if he or she is old enough to follow instructions). The dog discovers that instead of the reward of being fondled or even pushed away, he has the unpleasant experience of reaching toward a target that stinks to high heaven. This interrupts his learned behavior pattern. Most dogs learn quickly that jumping up is no longer enjoyable so long as the humans involved act consistently. As with so many of the retraining programs described in this book, consistent repetition is necessary to have a chance of achieving success.

behavioral problem by following the dominant-dog reduction program (see Chapter 3).

Have the device handy wherever the problem occurs. For example, if the dog jumps up when you return home, have the water pistol by the door. As you come in and see him about to jump up, command "No" and squirt water in his face.

Repeat this as many times as it takes to stop the dog. Eventually, he will come to associate jumping up with an

Right: If you plan to use the toy or ball retrieve method described on the opposite page, it makes sense to lock away all similar toys in the home. The dog will be very excited when the toy is taken out for the walk.

Retrieve toys come out only when it is time for a walk in the park.

Collar, Lead, and Hook

Though dog owners accept the need to use a lead and collar in the outside world, they rarely think of using it in the house. But most dogs are highly conditioned to the collar and lead, which has pleasant associations for them. Your dog will normally be happy to allow you to connect his lead and will follow you.

This powerful conditioning can be used to control dogs jumping up at visitors to the home. Ensure that the dog is wearing his collar beforehand. Hang the lead on an easily accessible hook on a wall or near the front door. When the visitor arrives, as the dog starts jumping about excitedly, clip his lead on, then choose one of the next steps, depending on your level of control.

1 Tell the dog to sit well away from the door. If he jumps up at the visitor, snap the lead and command "No." Now make him heel as you escort the visitor into your house. If the dog has calmed down, drop the lead on the floor, but leave it attached in case you need to exercise further control. After about 15 minutes, if all is well, disconnect the lead. Make sure the visitor does not fuss over the dog to excite him again.

①

Above: A collar and lead help control a dog even in the house.

Right 1: Training disks can also play a valuable part in discouraging a dog from jumping up.

Below 2 and 3: Just as the dog gets up on its back legs to paw at your trousers, throw the disks sharply onto the ground next to him while commanding "No." The clatter of the disks will startle the dog and should cause him to drop down onto all fours again.

①   **②**   **③**

Arms folded, no eye contact— classic Ignore tactics.

2

Discouraging Jumping—Recap

Methods to stop your dog jumping up at visitors include

Deterrents:

▶ **water pistol**

▶ **sound deterrent**

▶ **spray deterrent**

▶ **training disks**

Prevention:

▶ **Collar and lead attached to hook**

▶ **Snap on the lead coupled with the command "No"**

Left 1, 2, and 3: The Ignore response acts as powerful deterrent to stop this type of behavior. The dog is deprived of any touch or voice reward when he pesters you on his hind legs. Behavior that is not rewarded eventually loses its attraction, and the dog should eventually stop acting like this.

Be consistent— inconsistency breeds uncertainty in the dog's mind.

3

2 If the dog is uncontrollable, then connect him to the designated hook on the wall for about 15 minutes. Only release him if he calms down, and ask the visitor to ignore him initially.

Other Methods

Once a dog has been conditioned to training disks, these can also be used to discourage jumping up. See Chapter 2 on how to introduce the disks. The hook method (see Chapter 3) is also a very good training routine for dogs that dominate the house and visitors' arrivals.

In Conclusion

Whatever method you choose, remember that your dog is the product of his upbringing and of your understanding of his natural instincts. Obedience training, when carried out properly, is the solution for most behavioral problems. A dog that lies down or sits on command cannot jump up at the same time.

Different methods work for different dogs, so try experimenting. For example, use the lead and collar (my favorite method) and combine it with the use of training disks if necessary. Asking another person to help is equally useful at times, giving the owner a high chance of succeeding in a controlled environment. Wherever possible, try to predict your dog's likely actions and be prepared. You lead; he's led.

Useful Tips

▶ **If you wish to praise the dog for getting down, do so in a calm, gentle tone, not one that reactivates the dog's excitement. Alternatively, say nothing and carry on with your routine.**

▶ **Giving the dog a pat or stroke when he jumps up and then expecting him to stop jumping again only confuses him.**

▶ **Be consistent—all people the dog encounters and wishes to jump up on need to behave in the same way and to use the Ignore action.**

Dealing with Aggression
▶ Aggression Toward People

In this section, we will deal with dominance aggression and fear aggression displayed toward people as they are the commonest problems presented to me. Dogs are social animals, and if not socialized and habituated to people and other dogs, they can and do use many types of aggression to communicate their personality, mood, and status. The behavioral training programs I recommend generally apply to both types of aggression with a few minor adaptations.

People's domestic circumstances vary greatly, but the training programs I suggest are of necessity general in application. You must read carefully and select from the information that which is applicable to your dog and situation.

This chapter will be split into sections dealing with the situations where aggression commonly shows itself including: aggression to people, dominance to family members, aggression toward other dogs, territorial aggression, possessive aggression, sexual aggression, and aggression over food and when being groomed.

Dominant and Fear Aggression

Dominant aggression to people and especially family members is the problem I am most frequently asked to help with—quite rightly people take it very seriously. The second most common problem is fear aggression displayed toward people outside the family. Dogs can display fear aggression toward other dogs and dominant aggression toward their own family members—so identifying the problem can sometimes be a little confusing. So what are the

Above: It is important that a pet dog should accept handling by her owner without complaint or overt signs of aggression. The dog must learn that you rule the roost.

Below 1 and 2: It's fun to play tug-of-war type games with an energetic dog, but there is a danger that an incipiently aggressive dog will treat the game as a challenge that she plans to win.

①

②

main problems people encounter with aggression and their dogs?

Prevention Advice: Reducing the Dominant Dog's Attitude

If you have a young dog and wish to prevent him becoming too dominant with your family, then accustom your puppy or new adult dog to the fact that you are in charge by using the method outlined in the dominance reduction program (see pages 44–47). Most dogs do not usurp your authority and position as head of the pack.

Don't play rough games with puppies who appear to be dominant as this can produce a familiarity that may be difficult to undo at a later stage. Remember what the wild dog desires—leadership and a high, secure position. Leaders survive longer in times of stress or food shortage than lower-ranking dogs (or wolves). Obedience train your dog; this is the best-known way to control a dog and induce him to defer to your top-dog position.

Don't allow play biting in any form or pulling on clothing. Allow your dog to play with toys but insist on being able to remove a toy without a struggle. When the game is finished, lock the toys away so that your dog can see that you are the keeper of them and not he. Your dog must not win. Every game and obedience or feeding routine must have a set of commands and rules that you dictate. This includes a weekly grooming session so your dog learns not to object to your touching him whenever you wish.

Rope-type toys are popular, but this particular game of strength should not be practiced with an apparently dominant dog, especially where children are involved. The more the dog wins the tug-of-war, the more he feels confident about challenging the person playing the game. Dogs can then transpose this confidence to other areas of their relationship within the family—aggression may be the end result.

Below left and right 3 and 4: This dog accepts that her owner is leader of the pack and so can take ultimate possession of the toys. A dominantly aggressive dog may seek to challenge this position.

Warning
Any dog that shows aggression should ideally be seen by a canine behavior practitioner, especially if children are present in the house.

③

④

Circumstances: The Crucial Factor

However you view your dog's aggression, the circumstances in which it manifests itself are the most crucial factors that determine how serious the behavioral problem is. A dog that growls at its owners and the occasional visitor but never bites and is generally amiable is a problem dog and should be helped. But take the same dog and now place it in a family with small children who behave impetuously and who are easily within reach of the dog's jaws and the seriousness increases tenfold. It's still the same dog, but the "triggers" for aggressive responses have also increased tenfold.

Then take the same dog and place it with a single person who lives in the countryside and who has few visitors. It

Below: No one wants to own a dog that growls and bares her teeth at members of the family. It is usually possible to remedy the situation, but not always.

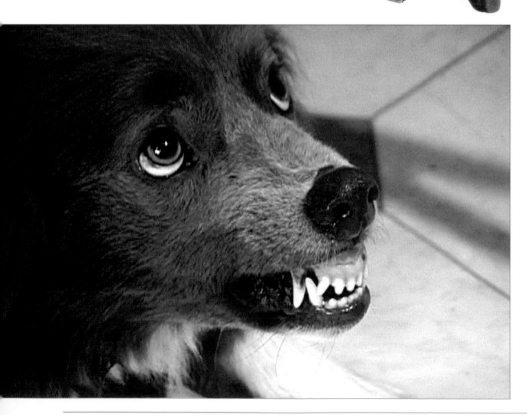

❶

❷

Above 1 and 2: Children are particularly vulnerable to aggressive dogs, but puppies rarely pose a threat unless something scares them badly.

may be the same dog with the same level of aggression, but the problem is now less serious.

So the circumstances in which the aggression is triggered are the key to its seriousness. The breed and size of a dog will also influence the seriousness of the problem: a Yorkie can inflict little damage on an adult with careful handling, but some of the large or giant breeds, like a St. Bernard, can inflict serious injuries even on the strongest adult.

▶ Fear or Dominance Aggression?

So how do we determine the type of aggression our dog is exhibiting? Body language is often helpful here. With dominant aggression, your dog will appear confident (tail erect, ears held high, body displayed as large as possible, and generally he moves forward to challenge, while eye contact is maintained). With fear aggression, the dog will look frightened and skulking (lowered head and body, ears down, tail curled under bottom—shifting eye contact and lip licking, which is indicative of unsureness). However, some dogs may display both types, being fearfully aggressive with visitors but dominantly aggressive toward their owners.

Dominantly aggressive dogs appear confident with a positive body carriage and the look that says "I'm ready for you."

The dog looks like she wants to run, but the fear may be channeled into aggression.

The lowered head and insecure demeanor are characteristic of a dog displaying fear aggression.

Types of Aggression to People—Inherited Dominance

All dogs are born opportunists and want to be top in the dominance stakes. Inheritance plays a part in determining how much dominance your dog will exhibit in your family. Very dominant dogs inherit a desire to be the leader, though upbringing, how you treat the animal, environment, and breed all affect his personality and the intensity of the dog-human relationship. Pedigree dogs often display more clear behavior traits; Border Collies may display an aptitude for aggressive chasing, while guard breeds may display territorial aggression, which is when a dog won't allow people to enter onto his property without imprinting teeth marks on their legs.

Puppies rarely exhibit true aggressive responses to people or other dogs unless unduly frightened. Their innate body language of appeasement seems to protect them until sexual maturity.

Dominance Aggression Toward People

So why are dogs dominantly aggressive to the hand that feeds them? Dogs are born with set instincts that prepare them for living in a wolf pack. Even when they're in a human family, dogs still assume their pack role and try to establish a niche through interaction with the other pack members, namely you and your family. Evidence shows that males tend to be more dominant than females, though there are plenty of exceptions to this general rule.

Dogs also inherit a predisposition toward dominance from their parents. The dog is often described as overboisterous and may pull on the lead or push through doors ahead of family members. Because the pack is very important to a dog, most dominant aggression is directed at other pack members.

The way you handle and generally interact with your dog deeply affects the dominant dog and his view of you.

Specific Triggers

Many people are confused by dominance aggression because their dog can be the most wonderful, kind, and gentle creature most of the time but not when he's eating, or resting, or whatever. They are describing a dog that has learned to be dominant in some, but not all, situations. In other words, the dog accepts your leadership in certain areas of the relationship but not in others. An example is the dog that growls only when you go near him when he's on his bed or eating. No other aggression may be displayed. That is what the dog has learned and gotten away with over time, so he holds on to it for dear life. It's not personal; just a dog behaving as dogs do. But it is still aggression, and that's unacceptable in a harmonious and trusting relationship.

Dominance Aggression in Public Places

In public places, dominantly aggressive dogs generally do not react to other people unless that person starts to impose on the dog by trying to pet or stroke him. Joggers and people performing other unusual actions, like games, can sometimes activate the dog. People who come too close to their owners to pass the time of day can also be perceived as a threat to the dog's pack position, and in such situations, the dominantly aggressive dog may choose to act.

I find it best when implementing the dominance reduction program to concentrate on training the dog to obey my commands entirely, removing from him this element of choice. He must not be allowed to make his own decisions on how and when he can become aggressive.

Above: Displays of aggression directed toward people constitute one of the most serious problems that a dog owner ever has to face. If uncorrected, such behavior can become a danger.

Below 2: By following the program described, it is possible to habituate a fear-driven dog to accept the approach of other people in public places. By using tidbits to reward the behavior you want to encourage, the dog will gradually start to allow other people into its "space" without displays of aggression.

2

Above 1: The body language of this dog says it all—the head and body are lowered, the ears down, and the tail is coiled under the animal's hindquarters. This is a classic example of a fearful disposition.

Fear Aggression to People

Though fearful aggression can be inherited, in most cases it occurs as a result of poor early socialization or an early trauma in puppyhood (see box). Most fearful dogs as they mature become aggressive.

▶ Possible Causes of Fear-Based Aggression

▶ Lack of early socialization during the sensitive period between five and 12 weeks of age.

▶ Early in her life, she may have experienced trauma(s). This means that as a puppy she has been traumatized, perhaps by a stranger. The cause could be something as innocuous as a person tripping over the puppy and accidentally hurting her. Even one such incident may produce a fearful adult.

▶ She may have inherited a predisposition toward fear linked to breeding lines. Some breeds of dog have a greater propensity toward developing a fearful temperament, such as the shepherding breeds and some toy breeds.

Fear Aggression to People in Public Places

Fear-aggressive dogs are very dangerous in my view because of their unpredictable nature. Common triggers are numerous: pedestrians that walk with a limp, animated children, well-meaning people in the park who try to befriend your dog by petting it. They may believe that this will rid the dog of its fear; in general, it has the opposite affect. Children of course are often attracted to pretty dogs, so you need to be firm and polite in explaining to inquisitive children that they must not touch the dog.

At this juncture, I will mention muzzles. It is best to use a muzzle if you feel that in the early stages of training your dog may bite or if you have not yet gained the upper hand in controlling him. The caged variety are best because the dog can still pant and tidbits of food can still be eaten through the gaps in the muzzle. It is imperative that the dog is taught to accept the muzzle in your home and yard for at least one week before walking the dog in public places. To understand how to get the dog used to a muzzle, see the training exercise on pages 32–33.

Keeping a Safe Distance

When you're dealing with a fear-driven dog, you'll notice that what triggers the fear in your dog is the distance between him and the object of his fear. If your dog remains reasonably calm at 10 feet (3 m), then that's the distance you need to start from when using some of the programs that follow.

If your dog is calmer in a larger space, then try to arrange for visitors to your home to arrive while you and the dog are in the yard. Always control the dog with a lead and collar or a retractable lead. The space reassures your dog that he can escape if necessary. Everybody should act normally and ignore the dog,

for it is direct eye contact or physical approach to the dog that triggers the fear reaction. If your dog remains relaxed, then your visitor can slowly throw a tidbit near to it. The distance between your friend and the dog can be gradually reduced until your dog is taking the tidbit from his hand. This will take many sessions and perhaps require many months of habituation.

Left: This is a cage-type muzzle. The dog can pant freely while wearing it, and tidbits can be fed through the mesh. This is helpful when you need to reward your dog for behavior that you wish to encourage.

Vaccination Period

▶ Another factor that can contribute to the development of fearful dogs is the recommended vaccination period. This occurs at one of the most crucial times of a puppy's life, between five and 12 weeks, which is the critical window of opportunity for socializing the puppy to the world he will live in—there is no second chance. At six weeks of age, I take all my puppies on short car trips. I park the car in a busy spot and just sit with the puppy on my knee (or in a cage) with the car door open, allowing him to see all about, habituating the pup to sounds, smells, and sights. I don't let other dogs contact him physically.

There is a health risk, but I believe it's the only way to ensure that my pups develop well temperamentally. It is your choice. Check with your veterinarian if canine diseases like parvo virus are endemic in your area.

I also invite people, especially children, and dogs that I know to be free of ill health to my home to accustom the puppy to them. Again there is a small risk—however the risk of aggression developing later on is a greater worry to me as it might mark the dog for life.

1 **2** **3**

Above 1, 2, and 3: It's a good idea to invite children to your home so that they can play with a new puppy. Socialization at this early stage of the dog's life helps her to grow up into a well-adjusted and pleasant pet.

Do Not Impose on Aggressive Dogs

One of the most important rules when dealing with fear or dominance aggression is to move normally and not to corner the dog or try to befriend him in the normal way. In fact, acting calmly and ignoring the dog completely often is the best way of reducing the dog's fear. Many people who enter a house as visitors feel embarrassed when a dog is aggressive, especially if they are dog lovers. They react by trying to win the dog over with kind, reassuring actions or soothing words. Of course, these actions exacerbate the fear, causing more embarrassment all around.

When I visit homes with an aggressive dog—fearful or dominant—people often expect me to perform magic and go straight into a hands-on relationship with their problem dog. Most quickly notice how I barely even acknowledge the dog. That is why I don't get bitten or provoke their dog's aggressive behavior.

The atmosphere becomes relaxed and calm, and I can observe the owners, the dog and his environment, and what is going on. People often say that their dog is unusually relaxed with me and better behaved than usual—that's because I am better behaved as a human and don't impose on the dog or owner.

Right: Because of the vaccination period recommended by veterinarians during which puppies are effectively insulated from the outside world, they can miss out on the valuable experiences of making friends and becoming accustomed to the world around them at the most formative stage in their development.

How to Remedy the Situation

Now we have a better understanding of how and why dogs behave in an aggressive manner to people, we need to adopt a program to demote the problem dog psychologically and at the same time implement practical training routines that quickly teach the dog that he will have to change if he wants our time and attention. From now on, it's you who should lead.

The main aim is to

1 Remove endlessly repeated commands of "Stop it," "No," and excited voice tones.
2 Use silence effectively to increase the impact of commands delivered that are clearly heard.
3 Stop owners panicking or becoming upset by their dog's aggressive responses.
4 Take complete control of all situations.
5 Train the dog to accept you as leader at all times.

If you implement the training program outlined below, remember not to slacken off when you see signs of improvement. This is a mistake and teaches the dog only to wait patiently to reestablish his alpha, or near-alpha, position in the pack.

The following programs, either pursued individually or in combination, will improve your dog's behavior.

Below: The dog must occupy the lowest position in the family pack's hierarchy if your will is to prevail. Aggressive dogs need to be demoted psychologically.

Above: You decide when toys and games are allowed. It's all part of the psychological demotion strategy.

Redefining Who's Leader

Psychological demotion is the key to all the behavioral changes we wish to achieve—it sets the ground for the practical training lessons to follow. Whatever the type of aggression you are dealing with, fearful or dominant, this program should be implemented for at least one week before you attempt to deal with the specific type of aggression. Safety is paramount in all retraining programs.

Get the whole family together, and agree upon a consistent approach. This speeds up the behavior change and reduces your chances of failure. All the adults and older children should occupy the top-dog positions in the pack. The person whom the dog already respects most should implement parts of the program to which the dog is very resistant until all family members can join in.

As you begin to implement the changes, some dogs' bad or boisterous behavior may worsen, but this is a temporary blip and as the week progresses, the dog should begin to respond. Other dogs appear (in their owners' words)

Warning

When young children are present, you should always seek help from a professional dog behaviorist or specialist dog trainer.

sad or miserable. Don't misinterpret these visual signs. This is simply the dog taking the cautious approach while the pack is rearranged. So now let's follow the program.

Days 1–7 Begin to deprive your dog of attention. Take away every pleasure that he takes for granted or that you may have unwittingly given him. This means no more strokes or free tidbits. From now on, every tidbit or reward your dog receives will be for doing something that you want.

Psychological Demotion

These methods are not punishments. They are ways of initiating a new regimen in which you are the leader and your dog is led so that he can learn how to behave. I find that even fear-driven dogs become more obedient and less aggressive when this program is implemented without dilution.

First, embark on a strict obedience course at a reputable club or preferably with a one-to-one trainer in the neighborhood. This has an enormous effect on your dog's perception of who is boss and your future relationship. All members of the family should take part. Then put into effect the psychological demotion program described in Chapter 3 (see also box right).

Ignore the dog when he pesters you like this.

❶ ❷

Above 1 and 2: *Showing him who's leader. No longer respond to your dog's nudges with a pat. That's now history. Rewards will come when you say so.*

▶ Psychological Demotion—Recap

▶ **Ban the dog from your bedroom.**

▶ **Around the house, make the dog get out of your way—do not walk around him.**

▶ **Give no unearned tidbits.**

▶ **Remove all toys and balls. You decide when the dog has them.**

▶ **Stop petting your dog "for free." Petting is now earned.**

▶ **Ban the dog from any rooms/areas of the house that he treats as his own territory.**

▶ **Don't let your dog though a doorway ahead of you.**

▶ **Teach your dog that he will get his food only when you are ready.**

▶ **Ignore any nudges or solicitations while you are reading or watching TV. Leaders ignore lower pack members.**

▶ **Let the dog into the den only by invitation, and make sure that he leaves the room when commanded to do so.**

How to Take Charge

As mentioned above, the first step is to embark on a training course, teaching your dog to obey "Sit," "Down," "Come," and "Stay" in all situations. The "Down" can present a problem for dominant dogs as this is a very submissive position. Take it slowly. If you are following the guidelines outlined in the psychological demotion program explained in Chapter 3, then your dog will probably be delighted to receive any praise. Use this fact to help you when training, and you'll find your dog will look forward to being trained.

House Obedience Training

Few clients realize that obedience training should be practiced using a lead and collar in the home. The home is where many of the problems with dominant dogs crop up, yet people will happily go off to a club once a week to learn training and may even practice in the park, but few teach obedience in the home. Practice three times daily using a collar and lead always. The dog can now see you asserting your authority in the place where he often feels more dominant—the effect can be immense.

Having trained your dog in basic obedience, you can then extend this control to influence his bad behavior. For example, when he will not move off the couch or when he growls when you try to move his food bowl, you can command "Come," then "Down," and then "Stay." Your dog will obey and will accept you as leader. This will take time, but it does work provided you are consistent and patient and are prepared to put in the necessary long-term effort.

The next step is to implement structured training routines that alter your

dog's ability to behave badly. In other words, stopping repetition. You will now decide how your dog will behave in your house.

Controlling the Dog in Your Home

The first action is to stop your dog using the entire house as his own territory with the right to roam anywhere, anytime. You will now decide when and what will happen—in simple terms, like a child the

Above: By combining time spent tethered to the hook with the reward of a toy stuffed with succulent meaty food, the dog grows to accept and even enjoy this very effective method of controlling him.

Right 1 and 2: Obedience training with the assistance of a collar and lead is not some arcane discipline that can be practiced only at obedience classes—get used to doing it at home too.

The dog is attentive to his owner's commands.

The order "Down" brings the right response.

❶

❷

dog has to learn and be aware of your rules, but you also have to rediscover how to teach them. Patience for the first five days is important. No anger, no shouting, no rough handling of the dog.

The equipment required is the same as that described in the chapter on the dominant dog (see pages 48–49); again you will employ the hook restriction program.

While you are at home, place your dog on the hook using his lead and collar for about 15 minutes a time three times a day. Condition your dog that you will release him only when he is quiet and relaxed. After 15 minutes, approach him; if he becomes over-excited, barks, or jumps up, walk away immediately. He may continue to bark or yelp. Say nothing. Ignore all remon-strations. Repeated many times over a week or so, the dog learns that you release him only when he is quiet.

The dog is now partly conditioned to a new set of rules that will help with visitors and on other occasions when you want to curb boisterous behavior.

The Food Toy Reward

It is very difficult to leave a dog restricted on a hook and lead and simultaneously to provide a reward that he associates with that restriction. By using his daily diet packed in a rubber food toy, you can achieve this most powerful reward. The end result is a dog that associates being placed on the hook with a plea-surable reward.

You will have to alter the type of food he is given. He will now get his food only through this toy. For several months, no food will be delivered through the food bowl. In fact, you can lock it away —but not his water dish.

I begin by dividing up the food up into enough portions to match the number of times I plan to restrict him on the hook daily. Three times in this case. Always use high-quality dog food. Poor-quality foods may be influencing your dog's heath and behavior. Do not use dry dog foods; we need real meat that is sticky and of a nice texture that gels to the toy.

On the Hook

Each time you take the dog on his collar and lead to the hook and secure him there, place the food toy on the floor. The more the food is jammed tight into the toy, the longer it will take the dog to extract it. That uses up energy, occupies his mind, and keeps him quiet. Over time, the dog will learn to associate the restriction with a powerful reward. He's also being conditioned to accept being tethered as a norm—just the same way he once accepted being restricted by a collar and lead as a norm when a puppy. After several weeks, most dogs happily accept the training lesson. You now have a good way of controlling your dog.

At first some dogs get tangled, so use a thick lead that will not feel rough on the dog's skin. If he barks to attract attention—completely ignore the dog and do not make eye contact.

Practice the hook method only when you are in your own home. Do not leave the dog unattended. Once the dog accepts the hook restriction method, we can now progress to dealing with dogs that show aggression to visitors.

Below 3 and 4: When you have taught your dog to respond obediently to basic commands such as "Sit," "Down," and "Stay," you have a powerful set of tools at your disposal that you can use when you need to assert your authority in any situation.

A hand signal reinforces the order "Stay."

The hours of training have paid off.

3

4

Aggression to Visitors

Dogs that are aggressive to visitors see them as a threat to their safety—they often feel trapped or view a visit as an intrusion on their territory. Dominant dogs often push forward to inspect or bite the visitor; fear-driven dogs can react with a facade of ferocity while inside they're trembling. Some dogs simply slink away or hide behind their owners' legs, watching as if transfixed by the visitor.

Controlling dogs within the home can be difficult, especially when you own an aggressive dog. What you always need to keep in mind is that the dog does not behave badly to upset you. It's not personal. It's just the way he has learned to respond to you, the environment, and others. A typical scenario in which a dominant dog reacts aggressively to a visitor's knock on the door and is "rewarded" with attention from both the visitor and owner is described and analyzed in Chapter 3. The remedial training method is also explained there. To recap, the stages to follow are these:

1 If your dog displays aggression near the door, then place your dog on the hook ten minutes before your visitor's arrival (if the visit is prearranged).
2 Answer the door, invite your guests in, and tell them not to acknowledge the dog at all.
3 If your dog starts barking, just ignore him. Make no fuss, and behave as if everything is normal.
4 Use the food toy packed with a part of his daily food ration.

Above: Dogs are very territorial, often sniffing around to pick up scent markers. They consider that your home is their patch and may react aggressively when visitors "intrude" on it.

Get your visitor to roll the toy toward your dog. If your dog is not interested in the food, he's not hungry. When the visitor leaves, don't make up the food.

5 Your visitors should not walk toward your dog or bend down near him. They should remain in their chairs. All visitors, whether children or adults, should avoid moving quickly in your dog's presence. Practice this routine with as many friends as possible. In this way,

Right: A dog that slinks away and cowers behind her owner's legs when a visitor comes to call may nevertheless behave aggressively through fear if closely approached.

you will build a good association of calmness, safety, and reward.

6 If your dog growls or barks at the visitor, never throw your arms around the dog to remonstrate. Do not stroke him or use a praising voice—also don't constantly say "good dog"—this diminishes real praise. Otherwise you will embed the aggression more deeply. If your dog sees that you are calm, his attitude will eventually be influenced.

Peace at last! The dog is concentrating on the toy.

The food is packed in here.

Above: *A meat-filled rubber food toy provides the perfect diversion. Your visitor can roll it to your dog across the floor, and once the dog has settled down to nuzzle out the food, the two of you can also settle down to enjoy an uninterrupted chat.*

Above: *Over a period of time, dogs that are restrained with a collar and lead can be acclimatized to the approach of a vistor—and eventually come to accept pats and strokes. The use of tidbits to reward placid behavior is a good idea.*

Common Misconceptions

When people give you the following advice, ignore it!

▶ "It's only a stage he's going through."

▶ "Dogs have the right to guard their toys."

▶ "He's only protecting you."

▶ "He's just a bit moody."

▶ "Just ignore the aggression and it will go away."

Training Disks

As explained in Chapter 2, training disks are used to imprint the following ideas:
• The dog learns a sound and associates it with whatever he is doing wrong.
• He associates the sound with the command "No."
• Eventually he responds instantly to the command "No" without the disks being used.

Timing is of the essence with regard to the command and the action of the disks being thrown. Eventually, you will be able to stop using the disks and to continue only with the verbal command, with the word "No" having the same effect as the disks being thrown.

Above: The loud clatter of training disks thrown onto the floor at the same moment that you order "No" helps to imprint the command in a dog's mind.

Many people read that you should never use any admonishment when your dog attempts to attack, bite, or growl at strangers as the dog associates this with the stranger. This is nonsense. If your dog has been preconditioned to pay attention to the disks and the word "No," then this association is already firmly established in his mind.

The disks and the command "No" work best when the dog is about to perform his aggressive routine. Once the dog is calm, you should if possible ask the stranger or helper to throw some tidbits on the floor near your dog. The dog is an intelligent creature and has no problem in discerning when you, the leader, are displeased by his aggressive actions. He will also realize that meeting a stranger can be a pleasant experience with the food reward.

Once you have reached a stage where your dog looks forward to visitors to your home or is at ease with people you meet on daily walks, you can begin to relax the hook method after about 15 minutes and release the dog in the den. Still allow the visitor to offer the Kong with food in it and/or the odd game with a toy—have the dog wear a leash for insurance.

Above: Training disks help to discourage certain actions. This is the other side of the coin. Small tidbits of food offered as a reward for good behavior serve to encourage the dog to repeat the actions that have elicited the reward. By repeated use of reward and reprimand, unacceptable behavior can be modified.

Right: After releasing him from the hook, it's a sensible precaution to fit a muzzle to any dog that has previously bitten or seems liable to bite a visitor. The old axiom "better safe than sorry" should guide you here.

If you are still very unsure or not confident, and if your dog has been previously conditioned to wearing a muzzle, then fit a muzzle to the dog while on the hook and then release him into the room. The guest can use pieces of chicken that can be fed to the dog through the gaps in the muzzle to maintain and continue the reward association training. In the park, you can also use the muzzle and food reward training with whoever will cooperate. Enlisting helpers unknown to the dog to meet you in the park to offer the food rewards is of great benefit.

Cage-type muzzles should be used whenever you feel your dog may bite people or while you are still trying to impose your control over your dog. Muzzles, contrary to the opinion of some ill-informed writers, do not make dogs aggressive. They do, however, make a dog look aggressive to the general public—that is a price you have to pay until a muzzle is no longer needed.

Changing Canine Attitudes

At the end of your behavior-training programs, your dog will have learned some new ideas:

- That you are the leader in and outside the home.
- That he will obey you the leader even in situations where he has become used to acting independently of you.
- A new language of training will have been learned with appropriate rewards and/or punishments when necessary.
- That people are not to be feared or attacked and that many people have tasty morsels of food waiting for him.

As time passes and your dog changes for the better, you will become more

► Euthanasia

This is the taboo subject for many dog owners. However, some dogs are just too badly damaged temperamentally for true rehabilitation to take place. As usual, it is not the dog's doing. I don't believe dogs are born bad. They may have strong innate drives that can run counter to human wishes, but that is still a dog behaving normally. We choose to own the dog—he has no say in the matter or how he will be brought up—so the responsibility is ours.

Most people will go to extraordinary lengths to avoid destroying their dog. Emotions run high, and facing reality is hard to do—to many people, it's like considering killing one of the family. Often people will do anything to avoid accepting reality and prefer to pass responsibility on to others—they may give the dog to a rescue center that can offer him only a pen and kennel for life. Not much quality of life there.

If a dog has been assessed by at least two canine behavior practitioners (not veterinarians) and the consensus is that the behavior is not manageable or cannot be remedied and is dangerous—then euthanasia is the responsible and truly considerate avenue to take. Your veterinarian will explain the procedure. Any assessments you obtain by canine behaviorists or a veterinarian should be in writing.

confident as you see results—the dog will notice you acting like a leader. Your new precise training language will be clear and consistent, and the relationship should flourish as both dog and owner respect the new pack hierarchy. As the pulling, panicking, and shouting cease and clear praise and rewards take their place, the dog's mind will become more settled and calm—I call this lifting the relationship fog. The result is a well-mannered dog, or at least a very well-managed dog, even if not always one that behaves perfectly.

① ② ③

▶ Aggression Toward Other Dogs

Dogs that are aggressive to any other dog, irrespective of sex, size, or breed, tend to be motivated by fear. Aggression toward dogs of the opposite sex tends to be of the dominant type and is stimulated by competition coupled with a strong inherited drive to be higher ranking and the boss. Either type can be caused or fueled by lack of early socialization with other canines. Alternatively, fear aggression can be caused by a traumatic experience when young. It may even be inherited—certain breeds are more predisposed to inherit a sensitive temperament and so need much more frequent socialization when very young. Fearfulness in dogs is quite variable too: some dogs are afraid of certain other dogs but not all, and some are apprehensive of certain places; others may have a combination of these traits. Some dogs are more aggressive when in a restricted area, on a lead, or in a car.

Above 1, 2, and 3: Aggression between dogs may be caused by fear or by a desire to show dominance. It's not always easy to distinguish between the two motives.

Fear Aggression

When your dog starts growling at or attacking dogs that it perceives as a threat and the other dogs back off, your dog interprets this as a success and the aggressive behavior is reinforced. Most fear-aggressive dogs are worse in restricted spaces and on leads, especially short, tight ones. This is because your dog senses a lack of space for escape and consequently feels more threatened. Conversely, some dogs are more aggressive because they are on a lead knowing they cannot reach the other dog.

I often find that if I suddenly detach a fearful dog from his lead while he's being antagonistic, he will look at me in surprise and his aggression will subside. Of course, it's difficult for the average owner to know why their dog's being aggressive, so **I don't advise anyone to follow this example**. Safety is always paramount, so use a muzzle on your dog if he's aggressive. It is also sensible to seek expert advice before progressing further as it may be difficult to identify precisely the underlying cause of aggression.

Some fear-driven biters can learn to appear to behave like dominant dogs, and often people have difficulty deciding whether the aggression is fear triggered or not. These dogs, in fact, have learned through experience how to remove the threat by attacking first. They seem dominant, but the underlying problem is still fear generated. These are often the aggressive bullies of the dog world. A good dog trainer or behavior practitioner can identify the subtleties of behavior in these dogs.

The Dominantly Aggressive Dog

Many dogs that display dominance aggression have been brought up in well-balanced homes and socialized correctly, but they still go on to become dominant and aggressive. These dogs may have been allowed to bully other

When to Take Action

Sometimes people instinctively know what they have to do, but they hesitate to do it because they lack confidence, knowledge, or determination, unlike their dog. Often many people are worn out by their dog's antics or just give up. Giving up can also mean eventually giving up the dog and passing on his problem to others. A quick consultation with a behavior practitioner can sometimes help bolster their confidence so the problem begins to be dealt with effectively.

I think the hardest step to take in dealing with an aggression problem is to admit its existence and to ask for help. I really do respect such dog owners. It takes courage for, by accepting the problem, you take on the responsibility of trying to correct it by carrying out advice that, though essential, might cause emotional stress in the short term to all concerned.

If you don't follow this advice, it may indicate to a dominant or adolescent dog that you are not in control. This may encourage him to assert his dominance further, and eventually he will consider his position in the pack to be higher than yours. The result may be that you or your family will be challenged with an aggressive response from your dog.

To cope with it, you must assert your alpha status by following the dominance reduction program in this book and training your dog in basic obedience. Following much of the advice on how to deal with the fearfully aggressive dog in this section will also help a great deal in remolding your dog's antagonism.

Always make safety your first concern if you meet an aggressive dog when out on a walk.

puppies when they were young or the owner may have an older dog that allowed the dominant puppy too much rough play without any put-downs—in other words, lack of dog discipline! Many dominant dogs seem to enjoy the cavalier action of bullying their way around the park and proving their strength. Fortunately, this type of problem is not as common as fear-driven aggression.

Above: The feeling of restraint of being on a short lead can prompt fear-driven dogs to shows of aggression. They may feel that their normal avenues of escape have been closed off and react with a sense of panic.

Next let's look in more detail at the many factors that can contribute to or exacerbate aggressive behavior in dogs.

Lack of Socialization

This cause of aggression is very common. It comes about because of poor socialization between six and 12 weeks of age and thereafter. This is the time when all puppies need to learn how to interact with other dogs and humans. If the experiences of contact are limited, the puppy becomes an outcast to her own kind—she does not learn the canine communication skills she will require to deter or defer to other dogs. Like children, dogs learn what they can and cannot do from play and general social contact. When these experiences are lost at the critical or sensitive period, they can become fearful and then develop the aggression that is the bane of so many dog owners' lives. Though dogs continue to learn throughout their lives, it can be most difficult to correct lack of early socialization.

Below: It's important that dogs learn the skills of socializing with people and other dogs at an early stage of their lives. Play is a powerful teaching aid.

Traumatic Experience

Being bullied or attacked by an aggressive dog can produce a strong imprint on a puppy or adolescent dog. Though many puppies can shake off such an incident, providing most of their initial experiences with dogs are friendly and pleasant, some individuals retain the unpleasant association for life. A very severe attack can create a similarly long-lasting impression on even the most stable dogs.

Some dogs can be traumatized by what appear to us as minor incidents. The fact is, it is the dog that reacts to the incident, not the owner. If a dog decides another dog is aggressive and to be feared, then the result can be the beginning of fearfulness of his own species. Moreover, many of these damaged temperaments often do not reveal their own aggression until some time later—even into their second or third year. But when it happens, they can grow more and more aggressive with each successive attack as they learn that attack itself can become a successful defence tactic.

Cyclical Aggression

Probably the most common reason that dogs become aggressive is as a result of being attacked by another. It angers me that owners with an ostrich mentality will walk aggressive dogs in places where they can attack others. The majority of dogs that I see have an early history of being attacked or set upon by uncontrolled, aggressive dogs. I have seen the same people walking in the same parks month after month watching their dogs repeatedly attack good-natured dogs, many of which will themselves become aggressive because of the trauma they suffered. These same people usually proffer so many lame excuses to explain away their dog's behavior or to absolve their guilt. What they don't do is address the serious problem. If your dog is aggressive, you have a responsibility to muzzle him first and seek professional advice immediately.

Possible Causes of Aggression—Recap

▷ **Lack of socialization when a puppy.**

▷ **Behavior influenced by a traumatic experience.**

▷ **Reaction to an attack upon themselves by an aggressor.**

This dog is tensed for action.

❶

❷

❸

Right 1, 2, and 3: Here a dominant dog is showing aggression to a companion. Such attacks can traumatize younger animals. Dogs that have suffered an upsetting incident like this in the formative months of their development may store up their fear and redirect it back at the outside world in the form of aggression.

The Rehabilitation Plan

How should we start to cope with the problem? At my center, we follow these procedures to test and assess the suitability of socializing dogs that are aggressive for whatever cause. If you can find a dog trainer or a behavior specialist who can show you by example how to do it, this is a good start. It may work straight off, and it also allows you to learn the introduction skills required. I use a large garden area that has a tall fence around it and enough shrubs to allow dogs to hide if they feel insecure when loose.

There is normally a dog trainer and myself present. The owner brings the dog on a lead into the area and relaxes for ten minutes as we all chat about the procedure. Sometimes we just sit on lawn chairs a little

Above 1: This dog is showing signs of fear that can spill over into aggression when another dog enters the equation.

distance apart to create a calm atmosphere. Next we carefully select a dog with a stable temperament that will ignore the aggressive dog completely. We release her and then assess the reaction of the antagonistic dog. If it is mild, we then perhaps use a muzzle and walk him about at a discreet distance until the dogs are reasonably relaxed. Sometimes we ask the client with the antagonistic dog to perform obedience training exercises to take their dog's mind off the test dog. This often works.

If the problem dogs are very large and aggressive and could be dangerous, we always use leads and muzzles for the first ten or so lessons and slowly work up to the socialization system described in the previous paragraph. Over time, if progress is made, we go on country walks with the dogs on and off leads. Other times we simply sit in a room with both

Above right 2 and 3: By getting the problem dog used to the company of a companion dog with a calm temperament, over time she can learn to lose her aggressive instincts and socialize happily.

dogs on leads to discuss the training procedures. The antagonistic dog becomes bored or starts to relax.

We have now reached a foundation level of harmony that can be built upon over time. The overriding factor is that the fearful dog realizes that he is not attacked and experiences the close proximity of other dogs in a positive way. Dominant dogs come to realize that they no longer decide when and how to approach other dogs. They also learn that we lead and are to be obeyed.

Time and practice are always the mainstays of these methods. In our fast-paced world, we often want quick results, but remember dogs are not instant—they move at their pace, not ours.

If you follow my advice and work hard, the following results should occur. I make no promises—but

Above: Leave the park immediately if your dog is attacked during training; one bad experience can ruin all your good work.

equally I tell it as it is. This is not a problem for which easy solutions are to be found—despite what you may read in other books and magazines written by people with precious little experience of the real world.

1 You will remove the problem, and your dog will begin to socialize with other dogs.

2 You will improve your dog's behavior enough to be able to enjoy a fair

degree of normality. But always be watchful and ready to control the situation if your dog shows aggression.

3 You will stop your dog attacking others while on his lead and prevent his making your walks a misery, but you will not be able to remove his desire to attack entirely or allow him to run freely with other dogs.

4 In a few stubborn cases, and especially if you live in an area densely populated by dogs, you may have to go home with your dog due to the poor-quality lifestyle with you combined with the danger he continues to present to other canines.

That is the reality of owning an aggressive dog for most people. The problem when trying to rehabilitate aggressive dogs are the dangers involved of a fight. There are no quick and simple solutions.

Below: With patience and sensitive handling, a problem dog's behavior will improve—but it takes time.

General Tips

▶ **Don't take a fearful dog to places where there is a concentration of dogs, like dog clubs or play areas, if you're trying to socialize her. This will increase your dog's anxiety, not lessen it.**

▶ **Don't use physical punishment with fearful dogs. It often frightens them more, rather than teaching them. (Distraction devices like water pistols or training disks are useful in some cases to interrupt the aggressive cycle.)**

▶ **Don't put your arms around your dog to reassure her if she becomes aggressive or shivers and shakes. These actions simply magnify your dog's fear. Taking a no-nonsense, detached attitude is better.**

▶ **Do find situations that don't frighten your dog, and do make use of dogs that your dog knows and doesn't fear. When you begin your retraining program, these dogs and places can be helpful. As your dog becomes more confident, other environments and dogs can be gradually introduced over many weeks or months.**

▶ **Do leave the park immediately if overboisterous dogs pounce on your dog and the owners either can't or won't control them. One overboisterous or aggressive dog could put your training back months.**

Getting to Know Other Dogs

I will now assume that we are starting with a dog whose belligerence is based on fear. What we need to do is to alter the dog's view of other dogs. This won't be easy; in following the program you will need to be methodical and *very patient*.

Firstly find some submissive, possibly small dogs, preferably of the opposite sex. I realize this might not be easy, but it's the only way. Start with one companion dog and arrange to meet the handler and dog on loose leads or retractable leads in a park or open space. Note the distance your dog will accept the other dog to approach without showing aggression. Then walk across the park, keeping this distance between you. Repeat this back and forth. If your dog doesn't bark or growl, lessen the distance between the dogs on each walk across the park. Never be

Above: Friends at last! There are ways that will help a fear-aggressive dog to accept the presence of others.

tempted to let the dogs off the lead because your dog appears relaxed at this stage. This exercise should be repeated daily until your dog accepts walking on a lead alongside the other dog without displaying any aggression.

Next you should arrange to meet in different parks and places or in your friend's yard, provided there is enough space to prevent your dog feeling hemmed in or threatened. Eventually—it may take several weeks or longer—the dogs should be able to walk side by side on leads without any fuss.

The next stage is to let the dogs off the lead. If you're

Left: Fear-aggressive dogs can be encouraged to accept the proximity of other dogs by a program of walking them together while gradually reducing the distance between them.

unsure of how your dog will react, then buy a muzzle and fit that to your dog. This will allow you to be more relaxed, which in turn will help relax your dog. Start by walking the dogs on the lead for around 200 yards (190 m), then release them and allow them to say hello to each other. If there's no trouble, you can build on this until they become good friends.

Your dog can now learn to play and interpret canine body language, and this will reinforce her confidence. You will now have completed the first step. You should aim to progress to meeting as many other helpers and their dogs as possible. Eventually, your dog may be able to play freely and comfortably with other dogs or at least begin to experience the fun of being with other dogs as opposed to any threat they pose. If at any stage your dog displays aggression, that simply means she's not ready to move on.

You may well ask what you should do if dogs come up to you unbidden in the park. Ideally, you should try to walk your dog at times when few dogs are about, and when you are walking your dog keep a head halter on it. You could also try asking other known park users to help by keeping their dogs away from yours, especially if they're dominant or boisterous.

The Leader Speaks

Training your dog to a high standard using the sit, down, come, stay, and heel exercises in a variety of locations not only puts you in control but makes you and your dog more confident with one another. We can use obedience training to prevent the first excitable aggressive displays by your dog and to distract her

① **②** **③**

Dogs Visiting You

Fearful dogs can be very territorial, so bringing strange dogs to your home can be a difficult situation to deal with. I suggest you leave this until you have first corrected or improved your dog's attitude in open spaces. When you have accomplished this, you can use a combination of obedience exercises and food rewards to introduce other submissive, nonthreatening dogs to your home gently. Follow methods similar to the introduction techniques described.

When using the above advice and training methods, you will find that all dogs will reach a point beyond which they no longer improve a great deal. It is for you to judge how predictable and reliable your dog has become, but if you are in doubt, a muzzle or a head halter are a sensible precaution.

attention from the other dog. If your dog is heeling, staying, or lying down, she cannot easily be preparing herself for aggression.

By redirecting your dog's habitual actions, you cool down the situation. You can then walk away casually using heeling methods and maybe give your dog a food reward when she has relaxed.

Above 1, 2, and 3: If your dog responds positively and obediently to the basic commands, you can use them to defuse potentially hazardous situations by reasserting your control over the dog.

Obedience does not make your dog friendly to other dogs, but it does stop the aggressive build-up of tension.

Food Friendly Associations

Using favorite tidbits is a useful way of rewarding your dog for good, nonaggressive behavior. This method works only with dogs that love food; alternatively, you could miss out one day's meal and on the following day take a bag full of chicken or ham chunks to the park to reinforce good behavior. This method does not teach your dog not to fear other dogs nor make him like them—it simply teaches him to associate a place where he may otherwise feel threatened with a reward, and that can be helpful.

You can also use food rewards when teaching your dog to walk in company as described above. Again, we need to use a loose lead or retractable lead. However, this time use the food rewards on each occasion that you meet another dog and your dog stays calm. Only give a food reward when your dog is not growling or barking. And, remember, repetition over a long period is required, not an occasional effort only when it's convenient.

Tidbits reward good behavior.

What to Do If Your Dog Is Attacked in Public

Every park user, whether a human or a dog, has a right to go for a walk without being molested by unsupervised or uncontrolled dogs. A dog careening wildly toward you might be friendly and have nothing more fearful in mind than saying hello, but its bulk and speed can be quite intimidating. However, you may be dealing with a fierce brute intent on terrorizing you and your dog. I've met people who have such a phobia of dogs that the prospect of walking across a park causes them misery. Though these are extreme cases, they're indicative of the fear that uncontrolled dogs can inspire. Badly behaved dogs ruin the reputation of the rest. If you fear being on the receiving end of an attack by an aggressive dog, read on for advice on how to deal with the situation.

When dogs attack other animals, they normally go through a three-stage process:

Stage One: *Predatory Aggression, identify prey.* Potential victims are sized up, and one is singled out.

Stage Two: *Predatory Aggression, pursuit.* Suddenly they take off at full speed toward their target dog.

Stage Three: *Predatory aggression, the kill.* The final stage is the actual attack. That's the wolf ancestry in your dog revealing itself.

Practical Attack Avoidance Techniques

If you or your dog is attacked, here are some suggestions on how to deal with the situation and defuse the crisis.

Before you adopt any of the defense methods that follow, do be certain that the approaching dog has aggressive intentions before you act, otherwise you could precipitate a fight when otherwise there would not have been one—your dog might be simply and correctly displaying appeasing behavior. An example is when a very dominant dog approaches yours and your dog appears frightened. You may feel that you need to rescue your dog from this humiliating or dangerous situation. By misreading and interfering, you can cause a fight. Sudden movement or shouting can activate the flight-or-fight mechanisms of the dogs. When they meet, dogs use a wonderful variety of body language signals that generally defuse tension and identify rank, sex, and age.

Above 1 and 2: When dogs meet, they usually go through an introductory ritual, moving slowly and inquisitively around one another, sniffing and sizing one another up. It's their way of establishing relative status without resorting to aggression.

Left: Don't always assume that big, fierce-looking dogs have bad intentions. Big dogs often have placid natures.

dog to flee so the chase can begin. By keeping your dog calm, disappointment will be his reward.

Object Defense

If the dog is very aggressive and is attempting to bite or you believe from his body language that he will bite, then try holding a solid object like a stick or bag in front of your body with an out-stretched hand. Don't be threatening or wave it. This display will normally distract the aggressor's attention, and if a bite does take place, the object is normally what is bitten. You need to appear calm and make few sudden movements while adopting these defensive actions.

Alternatively, you may have to let go of your dog if you feel that your personal safety is in jeopardy. In the final analysis, I can advise but not anticipate every possibility. It's your decision.

The aforementioned actions are not applicable to children when walking dogs. They really have to try and get help. Children should carry a screech type alarm for summoning assistance.

Passive Defense

However, if you or your dog are attacked in the park, this can be a very frightening experience, especially if your dog is small or timid and the attacker is large. In cases where the aggression is mostly vocal, simply telling your dog to sit and keeping your body between the two dogs will stop the situation from becoming worse. It is amazing how the aggressive dog will not come too close to a human to get at his canine target—circumnavigating an owner takes more courage than normal. (This will not work if your dog is also barking aggressively.) The antagonist might be expecting your

Below: If you own a small dog that is threatened by another in the park, you naturally want to spring to its defense. Stay calm and keep your dog under control. Your presence next to it is quite likely to deter the attacker from doing anything more than barking.

Umbrella Rescue

The most successful method I have found to stop dog attacks on you or your dog is a telescopic umbrella. It's called Defense Enlarge or DE. This method is now standard defense advice at my behavior center. The basic idea is that most aggressive dogs are not as confident as they appear. By carrying a telescopic umbrella on your person, you are equipped with a superb quick-action device.

If you believe that a dog is about to attack your dog, then simply activate the umbrella release button as the tormentor approaches, also pointing it in the direction of the attacker. The sudden pop of the umbrella will take the dog by surprise; keep your dog either on a lead adjacent to your body or hold him by one arm. During tests in more than 300 practical situations of aggressiveness, only two dogs did not either run off or just bark until their owners arrived and controlled them. The other two dogs snapped at the umbrella but never quite figured it out and did not pursue the attack further.

As the aggressor begins to bark, stand still and place the fully extended umbrella with its outer edge touching the ground. Then roll the umbrella

Above 1: *When confronted by a dog with apparently aggressive intentions, the handy umbrella can prove a surprisingly effective defensive aid. By opening the umbrella and using it as a shield for you and your dog, you change the dynamics of the situation.*

clockwise or counterclockwise according to which way the aggressor is circling you. The antagonist will find it difficult to bypass the defense.

The behavioral principle involved is based on the bluff principle familiar in the animal kingdom. We have all seen how some lizards expand their ruff around their necks to look larger than life when threatened by a predator; this trick works for them, and the good old umbrella can work for you and your pet dog.

Left: *A dog that appears intent on attacking you and your pet is a distinctly frightening proposition.*

Castration

In about half the cases where dominant aggression (not fearful aggression) is the problem, male dogs can be helped by castration. You will have to consult your veterinarian for advice if you think this might help. If the veterinarian does castrate, then this physiological change combined with a strict obedience and a socialization program should further improve your control over the dog.

Above 2: *Most dogs stop in their tracks and just bark at the umbrella—only a few try to pursue their attack and get around the edge of the shield.*

Above 3: *If the dog weaves left and right in an attempt to get around the umbrella, simply roll it along the ground in the appropriate direction to maintain the shield.*

Below 1 to 4: An automatic collapsible umbrella is perfect for the Defense Enlarge tactic. At the press of a button, the spring action opens the umbrella until it pops into position with a perceptible snap. The aggressive dog will be unnerved both by its rapid deployment and the size of the shield that results.

What Does the Law Say on Such Matters?

Almost 5 million people are bitten by dogs every year in the United States. Each day, nearly 1,000 people in the United States, mostly children, are bitten seriously enough to need medical attention.

Your legal liability should your dog bite somebody will depend on the city and state where the incident occurs. Most states will hold you responsible for owning a biting dog, even if you had no prior knowledge of his biting propensity. Most courts will award damages to any victim of a dog bite under almost any circumstances. Every dog owner should be extremely careful and also carry insurance that covers dog bites.

► Aggression Toward Other Dogs in the Family

Many people own more than one dog and, of course, where there are two dogs there is a pack and two animals who may well compete with one another for position within that pack. Packs are not democracies. A pack is a hierarchy with clear demarcation lines. Most people who own two or more dogs have relatively few problems as dogs are naturally conditioned to living in a pack. Dogs don't spend their lives worrying about rank: they enjoy playing together and feel secure in one another's company.

However, I frequently see clients with two or more dogs who complain that one has begun attacking the other "out of the blue." The situation can become serious, and severe injuries can and do result. So why do dogs become aggressive toward one another?

Hidden Currents

First, the situation rarely develops out of the blue, and second, an issue has generally been rumbling away in the pack for some time. Unfortunately, people don't always see the early signs of a dispute until there is a marked increase in snarls and growls, especially when the dogs congregate around you. In most cases, the aggression relates to you, the pack leader, and the privileges that one dog feels the other is enjoying. Jealousy is a good term to use as a general description, but it is not wholly accurate. With children one could simply make sure that both received identical care and rewards and domestic peace would then reign.

With dogs, on the other hand, such evenhanded treatment is normally the underlying cause of the dispute. Instead, it is desirable, for the sake of harmony, that the higher-ranking dog should receive extra attention and that the lower-ranking dog is aware of this. Dogs are not interested in human ideas of fairness; pack instincts dictate that they all have a relative position. Even within households where the dogs seem to be in harmony, there are subtle rank hierarchies which the dogs understand clearly. For example, one dog may quietly get up and move to different spot when the other comes into the room. This one may then take up the vacated higher-ranking position.

A New Dog in the House

One of the most common reasons for dogs fighting in the home is when a resident dog is suddenly presented with a new companion. Normally, when strange dogs meet in the home, a fight or similar altercation may take place, much to the owners' consternation. It's not a good idea to introduce a new adult dog this way—even if it's a female being introduced to a male resident dog, aggression can still take place.

When dogs live together in a family group, they have to establish a pecking order. This is normal, and in most cases, they

Below: Toys and their possession is often an indicator of who is above whom in the pack's pecking order. Fights for ownership can break out.

This tug-of-war is becoming a test of strength.

Above 1, 2, and 3: Owners should set aside human notions of evenhandedness and ensure that the higher-ranking dog in the family pack receives attention first.

can achieve their pack position by dominant play or by serious tests of strength, ritualized threats of aggression, the odd growl or snap. There are incredible subtleties going on wherever two or more dogs live together—most people do not notice the body language and vocal signals being exchanged between the pack members. Alliances can form between two dogs against another, but usually there is little friction.

> ### ▷ Causes of Inter-Pack Aggression — Recap
>
> ▷ **Higher-ranking dogs may become jealous if they see their owner, the pack leader, granting privileges to a lower-ranking pack member.**
>
> ▷ **• A new dog introduced into the home can create rivalries and pressure on the established pack hierarchy.**
>
> ▷ **• As young dogs mature, they may seek to challenge the existing pack order of seniority.**

However, as a young male or female grows and becomes stronger, it may decide to challenge an older dog or dogs within the family group. This often happens between about 12 months and three years of age. If the challenged dog decides to resist the pack climber, then aggressive fights can occur. Most puppies try it too, but this is not a serious challenge and older dogs treat it for what it is, puppy bravado.

Below 1 and 2: A new dog in the house often triggers displays of aggression.

One dog should eventually defer to the other.

Wolves in the Wild

It is worth taking a look at how wolves deal with pack hierarchy. Packs are begun by a male and female meeting, breeding, and rearing a family. The yearlings stay on through the next year and help rear the next generation of puppies. As time goes on, the pack grows, numbering on average six to eight members and sometimes as many as 40. The younger wolves tend to challenge the higher-ranking males, their brothers, and their sisters for rank, and in time a stable order is established. Peace reigns most of the time, and the high-ranking wolves are the enforcers as they remind the lower-ranking wolves of their place. Most flux in wolf packs occurs annually near the breeding season.

Wolves act out these complex behaviors without human interference. Your dog, on the other hand, lives in domestic circumstances that are alien to pack realignment and peaceful coexistence. I'm amazed how dogs actually do get on so well together, especially when, quite often, little thought is given to their natural behavior. An owner brings in another puppy or older dog and expects them to love one another and be the best of friends.

selves to live as one big happy family. That's a human desire and has no effect on what the dogs think. Honestly, you cannot force dogs to like one another. But this does not mean that we cannot help create the circumstances whereby any tension decreases and the dogs do get along. There are no guarantees, but most people do succeed.

Most interpack aggression in the home takes place when the owner is present—for example, when leads are being attached for a walk or when the dogs are being petted and stroked. At times like these, the dogs vie for your atten-

Above: If you do decide to introduce a second dog to the household, it makes sense to choose one that is not similar in size and breed to the resident dog. This helps to prevent struggles for status between evenly matched animals.

Left: Sometimes owners are puzzled why two dogs can live in apparent harmony when they are not around but start to bicker in their presence. The reason is that they are vying for their pack leader's attention.

Very deferential resident dogs, especially some females, do immediately take to another dog, but that is quite uncommon.

In the wild, some wolves are so harassed by other pack members that they leave or are ejected from the pack and peace is again restored. Very few dog owners see this as an viable option because they want their dogs and them-

Advice on Introducing a New Dog

Ensure your puppy or adult dog receives adequate socialization with other dogs; puppy classes present a good opportunity for this to take place. This prevents many problems of maladjustment arising. If you're about to purchase another dog, then look for one that is not similar in size or type to the resident dog. The greater their difference in size and weight, the less chance there will be of the dogs fighting and creating a stalemate. There are exceptions to this rule: for example, many small terriers rule the roost despite having a big dog as a companion.

Right: Strokes and tickles bestowed by the alpha pack leader are coveted rewards, and the dominant dog in a family will expect to be granted these privileges first. We often don't sense the undercurrents of tension and aggression that can affect the relationship between two dogs.

One dog loves this attention; the other is looking jealous.

approach. This speeds up the behavior change and reduces your chances of failure. Identify which dog is dominant—sometimes this can be difficult, especially when the dogs are in the transitional stage (i.e., the challenger is about to become top dog). Generally, the older dog will be protecting his position, although the younger dog may well be in the process of usurping that position, which means that you will have to show preference to him or her. You may well have more difficulty with this change than the dogs, who understand pack hierarchy, but change there may have to be if life is to be peaceful.

The look says it— "I'm top dog."

tion and one may feel that the other is pushing in—remember the dog that feels highest ranking next to you, the alpha, is not likely to allow another pack member to usurp his position. Generally, most interpack rivalry ceases the minute you leave the dogs on their own. This puzzles many owners; why should their dogs live, sleep, and eat together without conflict when they are not around? However, it does actually pinpoint the root cause, which is you and how you behave.

Right: Dogs are conscious of their status within the family pack, and whenever two or more dogs live together in a household, one dog will achieve a dominant position.

Restoring Peace and Order

How should you set about solving this problem of domestic aggression between dogs? First, get the whole family together and agree on a consistent

Removing Friction

Once you have established which dog is dominant and senior in rank, then you need to treat it as such. Whenever you are giving the dogs attention, make sure that the dominant dog always receives it first. This may seem unfair by human standards; however, dogs have no sense of equality and applying our rules will only produce friction. The same applies when handing out tidbits. In everything you do, you need to ensure that the dominant dog never feels his position is threatened.

Follow these tips:

1 Always stroke or pat the dominant dog first whenever both dogs approach.

2 When taking your dogs out for a walk, connect the dominant dog's lead and collar first and give him plenty of praise.

3 If the challenger attempts to push in, ignore him and continue with what you were doing.

4 Feed the dominant dog first—this includes treats.

5 Avoid whipping up excitement in confined areas, e.g., doorways and in the car.

6 Games with toys can be continued unless there is constant fighting over such possessions. In this case, remove all toys, bones, and chews for good.

7 When young children are involved, you must teach them not to overexcite the dogs. If a fight does break out, there is obvious danger to the children.

8 If the dominant dog growls at the approaching pack member, don't shout at or smack him. By doing this, you only encourage the other dog to feel important because you will appear to be supporting his challenge. You might even encourage fighting to erupt.

Take care when powerful dogs come to blows.

Young dogs will often challenge an older partner.

Above: If a fight for pack position does break out, it is generally best to leave the dogs to sort the matter out for themselves unless the threat of serious injury prevents this. By intervening, you may just be putting off the moment when the showdown has to take place.

Below: The dominant dog in the household should be fed and given any tidbits or treats before the more submissive animal. You should not rock the boat where pack position is concerned.

What to Do If a Fight Takes Place

If a fight occurs, you should, in theory, allow the protagonists to sort it out themselves provided the aggression is fairly low level. I realize this could involve injury and veterinary costs, not to mention the stress of watching. However, dogs do eventually sort themselves out, and when we interfere, we unintentionally prevent a pecking order from being established.

Another fight is then required to resolve the dispute. Very few dogs fight for fighting's sake. If there appears to be no end to the repetitive fighting, this normally means that the two dogs are evenly matched in size, dominance, and determination. One dog will have to be sent to a new home. That is being kind —keeping them both just because separation would hurt your feelings is selfish and not the behavior of somebody who loves dogs.

If you cannot bring yourself to allow the dogs to fight it out or if, for safety reasons (e.g., the presence of children), you wish to stop the fighting, then a clean liquid squirt bottle filled with water can be used to squirt a jet of water in the dogs' faces. Alternatively, a dog

Right: When two dogs approach you in the home for strokes and pats, take care to make a fuss of the dominant partner before acknowledging the more submissive animal.

stop alarm can be used to screech a loud wail in their ears. These actions can momentarily interrupt the fight and allow you to take control if you are quick. Of course, these are very short-term measures and do not remove the cause.

Left: Preferential treatment should be given to the dominant dog when it is time to attach leads to go for a walk. These little actions send signals to the dogs that you are aware of their relative status.

Canine Divorce

Remember that in a wild dog pack, any individual that is bullied or attacked can move a considerable distance away from the antagonist until the perceived threat is removed or the passage of time reduces the tension. House dogs cannot follow this behavior, so the dominant dog may feel constantly challenged no matter how many times he puts his fellow dog down.

Equally, if a wild dog is continually picked on and decides enough is enough, he will reluctantly leave the pack's security for good and take his chances. Again, domestic dogs do not have this option of removing themselves from the scene, which explains why the fighting is often so intense.

dogs is not a solution. When most of the recommendations in this section are followed, with regard to reassuring the dominant dog of his or her position, and provided you fully understand the reasons for interpack aggression, then peace can in most cases be restored within a few months.

Remember—tidbits go to the senior ranking animal first.

Above: By following the recommendations in this section, you can help your dogs to settle down amicably in one another's company.

A fight involving a dog this size is likely to be a serious matter.

Above: Constant challenges to his position in the home can wear down even the largest and most powerful-looking dog.

Depending on the severity of your dog's aggression, you may need to consider whether keeping him is fair to other dog owners and to your other dogs. A new home is a possibility, though it will be difficult. Permanently muzzling your

Advice On Reducing Interpack Aggression—Recap

▶ **Establish which is the dominant dog in your household, and treat him as the senior ranking animal accordingly.**

▶ **If a fight breaks out, if possible let the animals sort out their struggle without your interference.**

▶ **If you have to step in to a fight to prevent serious injury, use a water pistol or dog stop alarm to interrupt the fighting so that you can take control.**

▶ **In bad cases that just do not respond to correction, the aggressor may have to be sent to a new home.**

Left: The dominant dog will naturally seek reassurance from his owner that he is number one in her eyes. Make sure that you respond in the appropriate way.

The Pros and Cons of Neutering

Two males in the same house: castration

I have found castration to be of assistance in about half the cases I have dealt with. Alternatively, your dog can be injected with progesterone, a hormone that can lessen aggression. However, this is a hit-and-miss affair and not one I recommend. If you are considering either of these courses of action, then contact your veterinarian for advice. It is not wise to castrate the dominant dog in the group. Always castrate the less dominant dog—you may achieve peace by widening the dominance gap between the combatants. Take professional advice on which dog is the dominant one if you are uncertain, as the operation cannot be reversed.

Females: spaying

Recent evidence suggests that spaying bitches tends to produce more dominance rather than reduce it. Again, consult your veterinarian for further information.

The junior partner must wait his turn.

Right: This is the sort of scene that we want to encourage in the home—the two dogs are happy in one another's company and look alert and contented. On occasions, however, displays of rivalry and competition do not resolve themselves and a continual battle for dominance is the result. In these circumstances, unfortunately, it may be necessary to find a new home for one of the dogs.

►Possessive Aggression

Wolves in a pack spend a good deal of time collecting bits of carcass and bones and playing about with them. The odd bone will be taken and apparently treasured by members of the pack because ownership of the object is a powerful dominant signal of rank. In domestic circumstances, toys are used by many dogs for the same purpose of declaring ownership and status. This is especially true of dogs that have been allowed to usurp leadership of the family pack. We may regard it as a game when dogs try to keep possession of toys, but to the dog it's part of a display of dominance.

Right 1 and 2: It's fun to play tugging games with your dog, but watch out for signs of possessive aggression. If you cannot take the toy away at the end of the game, the dog is asserting her dominance.

❶

If your dog growls, snaps, or is just plain unapproachable when in possession of an item like a toy, you must understand that the dog has taken his dominance to the final stage and now uses aggression to signal his rights of ownership and status. This behavior is not acceptable in the pet dog for obvious reasons. Every time your dog gets his own way when he displays possessive aggression will add to his feeling of

dominance and superiority when he has the object between his paws. This can take the form of the dog growling when you pass nearby.

In the wolf pack, the frequent arguments over food are generally resolved through a set of ritual threats of bared teeth, growling, put downs, or stares. The pet dog also uses the same forms of communication with owners, but we don't necessarily see the more subtle signs. Owners that retaliate or threaten with undue force often exacerbate the

❷

The dog must learn that you own the toys.

problem—this approach is generally useless in the domestic situation. More subtle methods work better.

Possessiveness with Toys

If toys or, as is often the case, a particular toy is the cause of a problem, simply remove it completely, for good. Why

make life hard? By following the dominance reduction program combined with lead obedience training, you can alter your dog's attitude psychologically and through appropriate training.

You can, if appropriate, then reeducate the dog as to how the possession rules really work—you and the family are sole owners. Always using a lead and collar, throw a toy a few feet in front of you, then reel the dog in gently, and tell him to sit. Don't drag him in. Have some tasty morsels of cheese, chicken, or ham available. Offer the food simultaneously in exchange for the toy—the dog learns that this exercise has pleasant rewards and often the dominant challenge subsides. In time, the dog accepts the routine and food needs to be offered only occasionally until the new rules are cemented.

A collar and lead keep you in control.

①

②

The reward of a tidbit of a food is a strong inducement to let go of the toy.

Above right 1, 2, and 3: When training a dog to overcome possessiveness with toys, use a collar and lead. The dog should be encouraged to retrieve the toy, bring it to you, and then surrender it to you without complaint. A treat often helps at the final stage to tempt the dog to let go.

③

Using Spray Deterrents

Dogs that hide under furniture with a toy and growl when anyone approaches are most difficult to deal with. In the short term, I simply spray the air above the dog with citronella or some safe citrus-type spray—the vapor gently descends over the dog's olfactory system. This completely ruins the dog's well-rehearsed game of dominance, and he will leave the toy and the spot, allowing you to collect the toy in full view. You are now the alpha wolf. Don't say a word. It is important not to point the spray at the dog in a threatening manner. Imagine you are spraying the air with a room scent that your dog has probably seen you do many times. Your manner should be nonchalant, not aggressive. I've yet to meet a dog that stayed put.

Do's and Don'ts

- Don't try to take a toy back from your dog if he is underneath a chair, a sofa, or a table for he is more likely to snap or growl and you'll be in a vulnerable position.

- Don't smack your dog to make him release any object. Confrontation with very dominant dogs can cause complications or more aggression.
- Don't shout loudly at your dog. Use only clear, concise commands, and offer food in exchange for the toy.
- Don't kneel down talking gently to your dog as he growls—this only underlines the dog's dominant status and generally he will growl more.
- Do follow the Ignore method that works with some dogs. By not responding to his growls and grunts, the dog elicits no reaction from you. Some dogs stop defending their possession in the face of their owners' lack of response.
- If you find that the dog likes to take possession of items like shoes or slippers just to make the point that he has them and you don't, then spray

Below 1 and 2: It's obvious that the Spaniel is enjoying this game with a cuddly toy, just as the owner is. But if the dog's next action is to grab the toy and make a run for it to hide under a chair, the situation will have changed because the dog will no longer be deferring to the pack leader.

At this stage, the game is just harmless fun.

1

2

Dealing with Possessive Aggression—Recap

▸ **Implement the dominance reduction program immediately (see pages 44–47).**

▸ **Remove any toys or objects of contention if possible.**

▸ **Spray all children's toys or other items that the dog takes possession of with bitter apple or citronella spray.**

▸ **Resist the temptation of shouting at the dog—it only reinforces its feeling of dominance.**

▸ **The command "No" as the dog is about to take possession often helps.**

these items with a pungent-tasting spray every day. The dog finds that when he grabs them, the taste is foul.

Above: If the dog will not release the shoe, spray the item with a bitter spray.

Below 3 and 4: Now things are getting rather more intense—the dog makes a grab for the toy and manages to wrestle it from the owner's grasp. No problem there, you may think, but what if the dog will not let go when it's time for the game to end?

Eventually the dominance possession routine subsides.

• If a dog regularly finds items in the park that he won't let you take from him, read Chapter 12 on food scavenging and employ the techniques used there.

The dog turns away in possession of the toy. Game, set, and match.

3

4

▶Aggression over Food

Food is the strongest driving force for animals in the natural world. Of course, most dogs are happy to munch on what their owner provides on a regular basis and occasionally to supplement it with what they hunt (find about the home). Unfortunately, many puppies are not taught from day one that you have the right to take away food or place your hand near their food without any dispute.

This type of aggression takes the form of the dog either growling when you walk near him when he is eating or lying near his food or when you try to remove the food bowl that he has decided to guard in a display of dominance. In the wild, disputes over food are a daily occurrence, but they are acted out mainly through a set of ritualized threats —bared teeth, growling, or stares. In fact, the pet dog uses the same signals to communicate with his owners. Owners who retaliate or threaten often find that it only causes more aggression, which adds a twist to the vicious cycle. Each confrontation we lose reinforces the dog's belief that he is dominant and that he is the winner. This is the opposite of what we want. More subtle methods work better.

The following program shows you ways of avoiding such conflict and redirecting the dog's attention plus teaching him that your approach can mean a reward, not a threat.

Retraining Program

1 Change the food to a dry mix, which is less tasty and less likely to be protected than something more succulent.
2 Remove the food bowl when the dog finishes eating. Allow five minutes eating time daily only. This again prevents the guarding routine developing or getting ingrained.
3 Don't feed the dog in a narrow passage or a room in which you have to squeeze by. This only causes friction and unnecessary tension.
4 Feed your dog in a new area, preferably in the yard. In this way, there will be no food bowl for him to defend when you pass him in the house. The new yard geography also stops him from associating food with the place of former confrontation.
5 Allow no begging at the table, and give no tidbits at any other time.
6 If bones or chews cause problems, stop giving them permanently.

Obedience Training

Using the Come command that is part of the recall training program can be helpful in reinforcing good behavior. Use a lead and collar as most dogs associate the lead with control and are usually more respectful of their owners when attached to one. Then practice recall exercises in the house, repeated twice daily. This may take several weeks to master. The idea is to condition the dog to come to you on command. Always give a treat when calling a dog.

When your dog leaves his bowl on command, then you can stop attaching the lead. Your dog is learning to leave his bowl, to come on command, and to accept that you control the situation.

Above: Dogs that start to guard their food aggressively pose a real problem to their owners. They have to be taught that you, not they, are the master of the food bowl.

He also benefits from a food reward and realizes that the situation is not threatening.

Spray Distraction

This method works on most dogs if very subtly applied. If you have a very determined dog who always growls and for practical reasons you have to get on with your daily routine and get past the dog, then this method will interrupt the dog's guarding behavior. It does not stop aggression, but it stops the incident worsening or being played out in the dog's favor.

Use a citronella spray or other harmless bitter-scented aerosol. As you walk near the dog, simply spray the air at least five feet (1.5 m) above the dog's food bowl. As the atomized particles descend onto the dog, its olfactory sense will take in this horrible odor and taste. It is critical that you say nothing to the dog. It will generally leave the area, enabling you to collect the bowl of food quickly without a squabble.

Its important not to point the spray at the dog in any threatening manner. Simply imagine you are spraying the air with a deodorant room scent.

Food Exchange

This technique is used with some success. The timing and how you manage the procedure will determine how effective it is. Though I have used it on all dogs, it is especially good if a dog is in the early stages of food guarding.

First change the dog's diet to a less tasty one—dried dog foods often fall into this category. Follow the hook restriction program (see page 48) and using a six-foot (2 m) lead, attach your dog to the wall hook by his collar and lead. Prepare the dog's food and place it in front of the dog—just beyond reach. Then place some small pieces of ham or chicken on a plate next to you out of the dog's reach. Push the dog's food bowl within his reach and simultaneously show him the tidbit. If he smells

Above: If your dog starts to snap when you try to take away his food bowl, don't kneel down to reason with him—he may interpret the gesture as either deference or aggression.

the chicken or ham and prefers it, then the chances of success are high.

Simply offer the tidbit and remove the food bowl. This is called food exchange. This can be repeated as many times as necessary to teach the dog that

▶ Some Do's and Don'ts

▶ **Don't try to take a bone from your dog if he is underneath a chair, a sofa, or a table for she is more likely to snap or growl. You are physically very vulnerable in such situations.**

▶ **Don't smack your dog to make her release any object.**

▶ **Don't shout loudly at your dog. Use only clear, concise commands and offer food exchange.**

▶ **Don't kneel down talking to your dog gently as she growls. This usually reinforces the dog's sense of dominance while the close contact makes the aggression worse.**

▶ **Do follow the Ignore method that works with some dogs. When the dog sees no reaction to her growls and grunts, she may stop defending her food due to lack of response from the owner.**

far from being a threat, you are a source of tasty tidbits. Be watchful and have some help nearby. The tether will help prevent any serious aggressive lunges reaching you. If your dog takes to this method, repeat it over many weeks.

In Conclusion

Prevention is the best answer, but there are some very aggressive dogs that don't respond to any obedience training when food is present. This is normally because they are beyond mild correction or because their owners were not skilled enough to teach them at the right age using the right methods. With these dogs, the only answer is to feed them away from the house and so avoid the situation. You must be very cautious when dealing with this behavior, especially if children are part of the household. I do not think that aggressive dogs and children should mix permanently.

▶Aggression When Grooming

Why Dogs Show Aggression Grooming your dog ought to be very enjoyable—a form of social contact that the dog really loves. Most dogs do indeed like being groomed. But some don't. The problem here is that the dog is simply telling you, through growling, that he is high ranking, you are low, and don't forget it. Each time you groom him, he reminds you again. Most owners tend to get annoyed, but if the owner becomes aggressive and shouts, that just ups the ante. Expressing annoyance rarely works, especially with older dogs.

In my experience, nearly all dominant dogs that grumble when being groomed actually like being groomed. They simply want to reinforce their status in the only way they know how. In the wild, dominant wolves can approach any lower-ranking wolf and demand attention in the form of grooming. However, the converse is not so. Lower-ranking wolves risk being put in their place if they try the same approach on a higher-ranking wolf. Your dog is simply trying to apply the rules of the pack, but you don't like it and why should you?

Above left: When a dog first joins the family, grooming is very much about touch and physical acceptance of her human companions.

Right 1, 2, and 3: It pays to accustom dogs to human touch from early puppyhood so that grooming becomes an enjoyable activity that cements the bond between you. Take care if your dog seems inclined to snap when you brush a particular area—you may be hitting a sore spot that needs medical attention.

Left: It is satisfying to groom small, compliant dogs on your lap, particularly as the years advance and squatting on the floor becomes more of a strain.

❶

❷

Prevention Advice

Grooming your puppy daily for the first six months of its life, even if it is not a breed that requires such regular attention, while offering favorite treats (ham or chicken pieces) and making sure the puppy sees you as leader is the best way of preventing aggression linked to grooming developing later on. In this context, grooming also includes general touch, examination of the dog, or simply lifting her up and moving her around physically.

Right: Use a muzzle with a very aggressive dog, and keep using it until you are happy that the dog's natural aggression has reduced to a degree at which it is safe to groom her unmuzzled.

Breed Problems

More serious types of grooming aggression occur when a dog has a sore or injury below the fur. This needs to be dealt with by a veterinarian first of all. Moreover,

people who choose to purchase breeds that require hours of grooming because of the length or texture of their coats can have problems as knots occur and pulling them with a comb hurts the dog. If these dogs are handled by professional groomers from puppyhood, then the early conditioning of the dog to accept such handling prevents later clashes occurring.

Using Muzzles on Very Aggressive Dogs

Some dogs object to grooming by growling or snapping, but few dogs actually bite. However, if your dog does, then consider buying a muzzle while trying to reeducate him. You should accustom your dog to wearing the muzzle prior to the grooming sessions. This is especially important with very aggressive dogs, and it ensures that your dog doesn't have further irritations to aggravate him at grooming time.

Use a collar and lead to secure your dog to a wall hook, and keep some tid-bits (ham/chicken) nearby. Also make sure that the dog is very hungry—and I mean very hungry. Start by grooming a part of your dog that doesn't upset him too much for the first ten sessions. Because he is on the hook, you can use both hands, which makes your effort twice as effective and keeps you very much in charge.

Then slowly progress to grooming the more touchy areas. If your dog stiffens or growls, don't praise or reassure him. However, if he accepts light grooming, then praise him and give him a tid-bit. Do not physically pat your dog as this can be misinterpreted. Eventually, your dog may accept grooming and you will have mastered a useful exercise.

Stealing Food and Scavenging

Dogs are scavengers by nature. Wild dogs owe their success to their virtually omnivorous eating habits and their readiness to supplement hunting kills by eating carrion and anything else they find. To a wild dog, any food source can mean the difference between life and death. Domestic dogs have their food supplied by us, but they retain the instinct not to waste anything—whether it be an unguarded sandwich in the house or animal droppings in the park.

It follows that dogs don't understand our views on stealing food or indeed the concept of stealing—they merely eat what they find as their wild cousins do. So they find our reactions quite incomprehensible. Dogs learn by association. If every time a dog finds a delicious piece of decaying rubbish his owner chases him, grabs him, and tries to pry it out of his mouth, what is the dog to conclude but that the owner wants it for himself? Understandably, the dog learns that the best response is to make a run for it—and since he has two more legs, the resulting victory is a foregone conclusion!

Taste Buds

Dogs have different taste buds than humans and very different ideas on what is edible. Furthermore, they are not bothered by human perceptions of what might be unhealthy or dangerous. To dogs, therefore, the world is their restaurant. We, however, find it distasteful when our pets vacuum up waste food in the park or on the street. We also know that this is dangerous since it can cause severe food poisoning.

Equally, it is natural for dogs to gobble up cow, horse, and sheep dung or, in fact, the dung of any herbivorous animal. The dung of herbivores contains many partly digested nutrients, and the canine motto is "Waste not, want not."

Some dogs go further and roll in the stuff for good measure, perhaps to help mask their own scent. Again, humans are repelled by this. We understand that dogs can ingest some parasites through eating dung, but generally eating dung is more repulsive than it is health threatening.

In the Home

Food is the strongest driving force for animals in the natural world. Domestic dogs are fed on a regular basis, but they still have the urge to supplement this occasionally with what they hunt (find). This is frequently provided by neglectful humans who leave cakes, sandwiches, cookies, and other delights on temptingly low tables. It would be unnatural for a dog to turn up such an opportunity. Each successful foray reinforces the dog's instinct to hunt down such supplementary snacks.

Often, dogs learn to steal food more out of boredom than from hunger. Dogs

1

Above and right 1, 2, and 3: Dogs are great opportunists, and the hunt for food is one of the most powerful of their natural instincts. It is hardly surprising that a low table and a tasty slice of bread can lead to this.

2　　　　**3**

Why Dogs Steal Food

▶ **Nature—dogs are programmed not to waste food.**

▶ **Opportunity—food is left in accessible positions.**

▶ **Boredom—bored, lonely dogs seek entertainment.**

rewarding, a dog is likely to repeat it. To prevent this, it's wise to secure all bins, indoors and outdoors.

Some breeds are gluttons in the first degree—Labrador Retrievers are famous for this. Such dogs don't need an excuse to eat what they shouldn't!

Left and below 1, 2, 3, and 4: Where there's a will, there's a way. Dogs can smell food from afar and will eat what they find until trained otherwise.

that have been left for long periods of time with little stimulation seek to entertain themselves, just as we would if we were stuck in a room for too long on our own.

Following Their Noses

Their acute sense of smell encourages them to explore, and the exciting aromas escaping from the kitchen trash bin are irresistible. Tipping over the bin not only provides a food reward but also fun in the form of rummaging and investigating. Having found the experience

Obedience Training

At home or in the park, teaching your dog to obey your obedience commands is the only sure way to prevent scavenging. Since dogs cannot understand our views on food, they need to be taught that "No" means "No" and not "Maybe." It's advisable to teach puppies or new adult dogs the word "No" early on. Then walk your dog around the house on collar and lead. If he approaches any food, check him with the lead and tell him "No." It helps to leave food out in a container that allows it to be seen and smelled but that prevents the dog from getting a reward if he snatches it. This is vital, as one food reward may be remembered forever.

The rules are made clearer to your dog if you never hand-feed him and never offer food to him from your plate. Few dogs waste their efforts staring and drooling at the plates of people who never feed them by hand. It's natural to hand your dog a portion of what you are eating as a way of saying, "Let's share but don't take." However, what this signals to the dog is that whenever you have food there is always a chance of a reward, and this simply increases the likelihood that he will start helping himself.

Above: *It's tempting to feed a dog from your hand—especially if it's performing tricks like this. Tidbits are useful reinforcers in structured training routines, but otherwise try to avoid feeding a dog by hand.*

Deterrents

In my experience, deterrents are less effective than prevention. Some people recommend discouraging theft by leaving out food smeared with an unpleasant-tasting substance, such as mustard. This is usually a waste of time. Most dogs smell the horrible potion and steer well clear of it but still continue to steal untreated food. Others will just eat anything and look for seconds—treated or untreated.

Prevention Advice

Dogs develop the habit of taking food from tables or kitchen surfaces because of careless owners. It takes only one successful foray to establish the practice! The best prevention is

Left: Learning when "No" means "No." Teaching your dog obedience commands is vital if you are to stop her from scavenging around the house or when out on a walk. The use of a lead helps to reinforce the lesson.

never to leave food unattended. Lock every tempting morsel away. This will eliminate the reward and stop the habit developing—especially important in the puppy and adolescent periods, when bad habits are easily formed.

With a dog already conditioned to stealing, set the dog up regularly (see below) so that you control the situation and are not caught off guard. Allowing the dog to dictate training times is a recipe for failure. You must be in control at all times.

The combination of young children, food and dogs can be a nightmare for you—and a delight for most dogs. Toddlers often rain food down on dogs from their high chairs, and this is a difficult situation to resolve. Probably the best solution is to keep your dog out of the room while the child is eating and not let him back in until you have cleaned up all crumbs and splatters. If the dog has learned the "No" command, you can use this to restrain him—provided the child does not require all your attention. Alternatively, you can use the hook restriction method described in Chapter 3. It's important to be in control rather than let the dog dictate his own actions.

Left: Children love playing —and eating—on the floor. And dogs love them.doing it too—there's always the chance of snatching an extra morsel.

Below 1 and 2: A dog has to learn that his food will be delivered to him only through his feed bowl. You may deliver extra treats but preferably not from your own plate.

When offering food by hand, make sure that you call the shots.

①

②

Left and right: Those beseeching eyes and long, doleful stares while you are eating are hard to resist, particularly for people who live alone and rely on their pet dogs for support and companionship. However, when dogs learn that a particular behavior may earn them a food reward, the habit can become ingrained.

163

Left 1: Food left unattended is an easy target for a dog, especially a young one like this who has not yet been obedience trained.

Below 2: Sometimes smearing food with an unpalatable substance proves an effective deterrent, but it's not infallible. Some dogs eat anything!

①

②

Direct Action

When your dog steals food in your presence, the "No" command can be backed up with various aids, such as a water pistol or training disks. As he reaches for the food, squirt water at his face or throw training disks (or a large bunch of keys) just behind him. The squirt or the clattering noise will put off all but the most hardened thieves.

Alternatively, you can use a remote-controlled spray deterrent collar. (This is not a shock collar.) The device is very effective in interrupting undesired behavior like stealing food, although you will need to learn from a trainer how to use it correctly. The remote control means you can operate the spray mechanism without the dog realizing that you are directly involved—instead he associates the unpleasant effect with his own action.

Setting Up Your Dog

This "natural learning" method often has the best chance of teaching a dog what is a bad deal and what is a good deal in life. If you wish to dissuade your dog from stealing food when you out of the room, then "set him up." Tie several aluminum trays or

empty bean cans (make sure there are no sharp edges) together with string, secure the other end of the string to a piece of food such as a tough piece of meat, and place them all on a kitchen counter. Then leave the room. When your dog grabs the meat, he will pull off the trays, causing a terrible noise.

Most dogs will be put off by the noise. Repeat the exercise regularly, with variations and in different rooms, and a dog soon learns not to take food unless it is in his bowl.

Left: If you catch a dog in the act of stealing food, a well-directed squirt of water from a spray can provide just the sort of sharp, unpleasant shock that is needed to discourage the behavior.

Using Muzzles

In extreme cases where a dog constantly takes food (especially in the street or park where he may pick up dangerous substances), a muzzle may be necessary. Once a dog is accustomed to wearing the muzzle, he can go out anywhere without being able to scavenge. This interrupts the behavior pattern, and eventually, if this is combined with obedience training, he may learn not to eat what he finds. The muzzle can be used in the home for particularly persistent dogs or big strong dogs that are difficult to manage. Muzzles should not be left on dogs for more than two hours at a time, preferably less.

Above 1 and 2: With the dog held under control by means of a collar and lead, it is possible to work on the "No" command, diverting any lunges toward the plate with a restraining pull on the lead.

Below 3: Training disks add an extra deterrent effect. When you spot a dog about to snatch some food, throw the disks on the floor close to him. The clatter of the metal disks sets up an unpleasant association in the dog's mind with the act of stealing the food.

▶ Recap

▶ • **Don't leave food unattended or within the dog's reach.**

▶ • **Work on the "No" command.**

▶ • **Don't offer tidbits from your plate.**

▶ • **Make stealing an unpleasant experience (use a water pistol, training disks, or "set up" situations with clattering trays).**

▶ • **Dedicated thieves and scavengers may need a muzzle—for short periods only.**

▶ Sexual Problems

Very few dogs are genuinely oversexed. Overtly sexual behaviour, such as mounting cushions or people's legs, is not uncommon in puppies and is a natural part of adolescence with its surge of hormones. Mounting another dog is also an assertion of dominance and one of the means by which a pup establishes his position among its littermates.

Most pups will outgrow inappropriate mounting behavior. However, some — most commonly males, but also some bitches—develop this habit to an unacceptable level and continue it into adulthood. Most owners find it embarrassing to own a dog with a sexual fixation on cushions or a favorite cuddly toy. When dogs direct their attentions to human arms and legs, this is even more objectionable and potentially dangerous where children or the elderly are concerned.

Marking Territory

An associated unpleasant habit that some dogs develop is lifting a leg on furniture—or even on human legs. Although this may not necessarily be related to sexual behavior, it can be discouraged by using some of the same methods, as outlined below.

▶ Prevention Advice

Water Pistol and Training Disks

One simple deterrent is a water pistol (or a plastic bottle filled with water). As soon as you see your dog start to mount a cushion, etc., squirt a jet of water at him, with the command "No." Aim the jet at his face—most dogs' bodies are too well covered with fur for a squirt to have much effect. If your dog has already been conditioned to the use of training disks, you can use these instead of a water pistol. Repeat the treatment

Above: This is the moment that many dog owners dread—a visitor has just arrived at the house and your dog decides to relieve his sexual urges on his leg. It is embarrassing when directed at an adult but potentially dangerous when small children or the elderly and infirm are targets.

every time the dog indulges in the undesirable behavior, and eventually the command "No" should be enough to stop him in his tracks on its own.

Redirect the Energy

If your dog loves playing with a favorite ball or toy, teach him to fetch it. Reward him with praise each time he brings the ball back and repeat the exercise two or three times daily. Keep the sessions short —never continue until he is bored or tired.

When the ball's appearance or the command "Fetch" produces an immediate response from your dog, his training has progressed sufficiently to be of use as a distraction from the undesired activity. Now if you see your dog about to mount somebody or something, call his name in an excited voice, and throw the ball. In this way, his mind is diverted to the ball game and away from sexual gratification.

Scent and Taste Deterrents

Dogs that mount people's arms or legs can be discouraged by spraying the

Left: Someone tell the dog that this is a cuddly toy, not a mate! Young dogs are prone to act like this as their bodies respond to hormonal urges.

in the owner pouncing, shrieking, or even smacking, it's all attention—which such dogs construe as a reward. In such cases, leaving the room each time the dog starts can result in a cessation of the behavior. So apply your chosen method with this in mind, and stick to the one that works for you.

Below: If you are dealing with a dog that persistently mounts a person's arms or legs, it often helps to spray that person's limbs with a bitter-smelling (but harmless) spray. It's a useful method to use where children are concerned as they may tend to panic when confronted by an unruly dog.

appropriate body parts with a scent or taste deterrent, like lemon or citronella spray. This is a particularly useful method to protect small children, who are likely to have difficulty controlling a dog by voice. Spray deterrents can also be used to protect objects such as cushions. Reapply the spray three times a day for a week. The dog will soon learn that his sexual targets offer an unpleasant, rather than a rewarding, experience. This method is often very effective.

Obedience Training

Last, but not least, obedience train your dog. When he is trained to a sufficiently high standard, you can use the sit, down, and stay commands to divert your dog's attention as soon as he starts to mount something, rewarding him when he obeys.

In Conclusion

Some dogs (especially bouncy, dominant ones) use inappropriate sexual behavior as a means of actively seeking attention. If mounting a cushion results

---

Recap

▶ **Active deterrent—water pistol or training disks.**

▶ **Passive deterrent—deterrent spray on object.**

▶ **Redirection—ball game and/or obedience training.**

▶ **Avoidance of reward—leave the room.**

Should I Neuter My Dog?

Many people consider neutering as an option to prevent male dogs exhibiting undesirable sexual behaviour. In serious cases, you should consult your veterinarian regarding neutering, which does in many cases stop or reduce sexual impulses. I am not in favor of chemical castration as I have seen very poor results from this approach.

Castration

Male dogs, like the males of most mammal species, are driven by their instincts and hormones to reproduce with any female in heat (estrus) in their vicinity. For some reason, it's comparatively uncommon for owners to neuter male dogs as opposed to spaying bitches. Castration often, but not always, makes a male dog a better household companion. It also has some health benefits. It has been argued that if all nonbreeding male dogs were castrated, the amount of dominant aggression displayed by dogs to people and other dogs would reduce considerably. This is probably so, though much of this type of aggression could be prevented in any

①

case by educating owners on how to socialize young male puppies at the sensitive preadolescent stage.

Prevention of Dominant Aggression

There are circumstances when castrating dogs is recommended. One instance is when a behavior practitioner, in conjunction with a veterinarian, feels that neutering will reduce aggressive or dominant behavior. When the testicles are removed, the amount of the male hormone testosterone in the dog's body is greatly reduced. This consequently reduces competitive and/or related sexually aggressive behavior, though it can take up to six months for the full effects to be noticed. Castration works best on younger dogs.

Hypersexuality

Castration may also be advisable for oversexed dogs. Hypersexual behavior is not uncommon in adolescent male dogs, when it is caused by occasional hormone surges and will usually settle down with maturity. But when a dog continues into adulthood with an excessive desire to mount anything that moves, this can be a serious nuisance. It may also be accompanied by aggression, especially where children are involved. In such cases, it is worth considering

Above: *Persistent mounting of cushions and toys can be a way of soliciting attention. In such instances, it is best to ignore the dog and leave the room.*

castration. Of course, do take advice from your veterinarian and also from a canine behavior practitioner.

Causes of Hypersexuality:
- Hormonal surges
- Habitual learned behavior
- Sexually driven dominance

The effects of neutering are usually not apparent for some time. In my experience, a considerable reduction of sexual behavior usually takes place within four weeks, followed by a further gradual reduction over some months—although this can vary. Castration is not a cure-all for all male bad habits and is often carried out unnecessarily in the hope that it will have an effect, rather than as a result of a rational assessment of the behavioral problem.

The most common question I am asked about castration is whether it will make a dog less masculine and alter his

A squirt in the face has the most effect.

When the water pistol technique is accompanied by the firm command "No," the dog starts to learn that this is not acceptable to you.

2

3

Neutering a Male Dog—Pros and Cons

▶ When you buy a puppy, some breeders may request that you do not have him neutered. However, if there is good reason to do so, that should override the breeder's interest.

▶ Castration has little effect on a dog's aggression if he is already an established fighter with other dogs.

▶ Castrated dogs are prone to put on weight if their diet isn't carefully watched.

▶ Neutered dogs may urine-mark territory less often, but castration will not necessarily cure a dog who is in the habit of lifting a leg on furniture.

▶ Castration usually has a calming effect on general behavior.

▶ Castrated dogs are less likely to roam.

Above 1, 2, and 3: When large and powerful adolescent dogs display hypersexual behavior, they present quite a formidable challenge. The use of a water pistol or spray can be extremely effective in stopping them in their tracks.

character. My answer to this is: yes, his character and behavior will change, otherwise there would be no point to the operation. However, his basic personality will remain more or less the same. Probably the greatest change you will see will be the fact that he may not be as stimulated in certain situations.

Right: Castration will often calm oversexed dogs, but seek professional advice about it.

House Toilet Training

Most people realize when they acquire a new dog that they will have to invest time in training him. House training comes at the top of the list for obvious reasons, especially where young children are present, and it's critical to establish some ground rules from day one. Nobody wants to play hopscotch around their rooms while avoiding dog mess!

Dogs usually become housebroken naturally as long as they are given the opportunity to defecate and urinate in the right area. However, we often expect too much too quickly, and that is where problems begin.

Patience is all-important. When a puppy messes in the house, it's no use scolding him, smacking him or, even

Above: *Puppies enter the world with their dog instincts intact but with no idea of what humans will expect of them. Messes on the carpet are unavoidable.*

worse, rubbing his nose in the mess. He won't associate the punishment with the "crime"—all he will learn is to be wary of his owner. In fact, repeated punishments, verbal or physical, can make some dogs so stressed that they mess more often than before.

Even if you punish your dog when you catch him in the act, this may only teach him that it is wrong to mess in your presence since the same deed goes unpunished when you are not there. Alternatively, he may learn that you don't like him messing in one particular room and respond by selecting a different room or a less conspicuous place —not the desired effect at all. Unfortunately for puppies, teaching owners to "think dog" can be harder than teaching a puppy to be clean.

The New Puppy

When a puppy enters your home, like a human infant, he has to empty his bladder and bowels frequently, and he has no inborn desire to keep your house clean. When you start teaching him, he still has no idea what it is all about, and his mental and physical capacity to learn, remember, and associate is limited. By the time he realizes that you are his new pack and the house is his territory, he has often already made many smelly mistakes if you haven't taken the necessary precautions.

Puppies and adult dogs in the wild are naturally clean in their dens— nature's precaution against disease. A wolf cub, for instance, will wobble over to the nearest dung deposit area to leave his calling card. The presence of adult wolves ensures that smell indicators are in place to guide him. In your home, no such natural indications are present, no signposts, just lovely big carpets, linoleum, or floor tiles.

Stage 1 Training

The surest way to teach housebreaking quickly and consistently is to deny the puppy the opportunity to set up smelly "signposts" around the house. Instead of giving the new arrival the run of the house, restrict him initially to a limited area, either using a large playpen or fencing off a set area. If possible, choose a room with a hard, easy-clean floor (no carpets!) and ideally with access to the outside world.

Line the whole room with newspapers, and pop the puppy's pen, with his bed in it, in one corner. While in the pen, he has no choice but to relieve himself on the papers. You can speed matters up by remembering that puppies need to relieve themselves immediately after they wake up and

also after each meal. So, if possible, at these times always take your puppy to an outside area for toilet training and wait until he empties his bowels, praising him when he does so. We have now begun a two-area training program. The pup can be placed safely in the pen when you are not about and roam free outside the pen in the newspaper-covered room when you are present.

Toys and chews should be made available whenever the puppy is left alone in his pen. I find large raw marrow bones are the most attractive to a puppy. Plastic imitation ones don't have the same fascination as real bone. Don't use any other type of bones, especially chicken bones, as these can splinter and cause internal injury.

This program ensures that the puppy never has the chance to make a mess in the wrong place. He is gradually conditioned to learn that he can defecate on paper, often scented with urine to encourage him, and outside in the yard, where natural smells are in abundance. Eventually, he will seek out one or other of these places when he needs them.

2

Above 1, 2, and 3: By using newspapers spread on the floor of a specific room when a puppy is introduced to a house, he can become habituated to the idea of relieving himself either on the newspaper or outside in the yard when you let him out. Gradually, the papered area can be reduced and finally moved outside into the yard.

3

171

Stage 2 Training

When your puppy is about 14 weeks old (assuming he arrived at about eight weeks) you can remove the pen or barrier and give him full freedom of the room. Now reduce the newspapers until they cover about half the floor, and move the dog's bed to one corner of the room, away from the papers. He should naturally use the reduced paper area on the floor, as that is what he has been conditioned to do in his short life. If he makes a few mistakes in the wrong area, go back to covering the whole floor with papers again for a few more weeks.

After several more weeks, gradually move the papers nearer the doorway (if that leads to a yard) and then outside the door (weighted down to stop them

blowing away). Your dog will now look for the papers to relieve himself or have already gained a preference for the yard itself. Most dogs, when given the opportunity, prefer to excrete on soil or concrete areas rather than indoors, where floors often smell of chemical cleaning agents. A dog door fitted to a door will also encourage the dog to leave the room into the yard if he needs to defecate or urinate.

Remember to praise your pup whenever he defecates or urinates in the right place. A secondary command like "Hurry up" often helps to teach the animal that his action pleases you and is handy for future use when curb training. Many dogs learn through this type of command to toilet on command, which is very handy.

Stage 3 Training

Once a puppy is relieving himself outside the home in an appropriate area—preferably in your own yard or garden so that you can clean the mess up—you can start to open the house up slowly

and allow him to investigate the rooms one by one. You may still leave a small area of papers in the original room for emergencies.

Some people ask how they are to form a relationship with a puppy if he is kept in isolation. The answer is that confinement should not equal isolation. Choose a room that you and your family will frequent regularly, and make time to play with the puppy in his special room. You also have visits to the yard and walk times to bond with your pup. Puppies tend to sleep about 18 hours a day, so normal contact is available if one makes the effort. As time goes on, the puppy will soon be allowed into more of your home.

Indoor Cages

The pen method described previously is useful, especially from a safety and training point. However, for puppies over 14 weeks or difficult adult dogs that have not successfully learned the paper method, you will have little choice but

Above: Be prepared! Puppies always need to relieve themselves when they wake up and after meals.

Below: It is a good idea to praise your puppy when he relieves himself on the newspaper as you want him to do. The reward of your encouragement helps to imprint the behavior that you want to reinforce. Add a command like "Hurry up" for future use.

Above: Puppies can be placed safely in an indoor pen while you are out of the house.

to use an indoor cage. This should be big enough for your dog to stand and lie down comfortably. This method makes use of the fact that dogs do not like relieving themselves in their own sleeping area. They generally select an area nearby but not actually where they eat or sleep.

You will need to accustom the dog to the cage first, otherwise he will find confinement stressful and you could have problems with barking and whining. Start by feeding the dog in the cage, with the door open, and encouraging him to take his toys in. This ensures that his first impression is positive. After a few more days, when he should be comfortable with the cage, try closing the cage door while you are busy about the room. If he whines, ignore him—say nothing and offer no eye contact. The next stage is to leave the dog in the cage with a tasty treat or chew for a short while, building up to half-hour sessions. Repeat this action several times daily. When releasing him

from the cage, don't fuss or praise him—we don't want the dog to see getting out of the cage as a rewarding experience, rather to regard the cage as something normal.

The Cage Solution

When the dog fully accepts half-hour sessions in the cage, then begin your toilet-training program within it. If a dog messes indoors only during the night, then use the cage only at night.

Remember that puppies cannot last all night without relieving themselves, so make sure the cage is big enough to place newspaper in one half. This should not apply to adult dogs, as they have mature bladder control.

Each time you feed your dog or he wakes up, allow him immediate access to the designated toilet area, either the yard or the newspaper area. At night, or when you are not there, place your dog in the indoor pen. He won't want to soil his sleeping area, so remember when you let him out that he will probably want to relieve himself at once.

In this way, your dog will learn to hold himself for set periods of time and to form a routine of going to his toilet area when he is released and being praised for doing so.

Left: An indoor cage can be useful in toilet training. Dogs do not like to soil the area in which they sleep, so they will learn to contain themselves until let out, when they can be directed to a chosen toilet area.

If Separation Anxiety Is the Cause

Separation anxiety can cause house-training problems, especially in adult dogs. Dogs suffering from this often pace the room. They sometimes chew or bark and exhibit other displacement behaviors. This activity and the stress of being separated from their owner can make them defecate and/or urinate in the house.

If your dog is one of this type, you need to consider reducing the amount of attention he receives, including petting and play, by at least half, especially if the dog constantly follows you about or solicits excessive attention. Just before leaving your dog, withdraw all attention to help to prepare the dog for your departure. Do the same on your return, taking a "no big deal" approach, and do not respond to your dog's displays of wild excitement. If you can gradually reduce the dog's anxiety during your absence, this will tackle the house-training problem. See Chapter 5 on Separation Anxiety for more detailed guidance.

Territory Marking by Male Dogs

Dominant dogs sometimes mark their territory by squirting urine about the house, especially on furnishings. This has nothing to do with any need to urinate: it's just an instinctive territorial habit, and the more dominant a dog, the more it may happen. They often do this if new people or other dogs visit their territory (home) or when they themselves visit other people's houses—leaving a calling card is what wild dogs do when roaming about. I've even had several urinate on my leg in the blink of an eye while I was talking to their owners. It's not personal. They are just letting you know that they are important and here. The dog lifts his leg high to leave the

Right: Dogs respond to the scent of urine that is sprayed around their "patch" by other dogs who want to assert territorial dominance. Dominant dogs sometimes take to spraying items of furniture around the house in the same way.

Ignore his pestering.

The dog wants your attention.

> ### What's My Dog's Problem?
>
> **Dogs make a mess indoors for one of the following reasons:**
>
> ▶ **House training was not carried out correctly. Start again from scratch.**
>
> ▶ **The dog suffers from separation anxiety. Tackle the source problem.**
>
>   ▶ **A dominant male is territory marking. Try deterrent sprays on furniture, and consider castration.**

Left: This dog is anticipating that his owner is about to leave the house and is saying, "I don't want to be alone." Separation anxiety can lead to a number of nuisance behaviors including incontinence around the home. You must accustom the dog to periods of solitude by ignoring his attention-seeking strategies.

Useful Tips

▶ **Use several layers of newspapers on the floor so that the bottom layer stays more or less dry.**

▶ **There are some commercial sprays that help direct a puppy to the paper. I find blotting a little of the puppy's own urine on to the paper just as effective.**

▶ **Never punish a puppy for urinating or defecating—all this achieves is to spoil his temperament.**

▶ **It is better to reward a puppy for messing in the right place than to scold him for wrongdoing.**

Below: You will inevitably have to clear up dog mess while house training your dog. Pooper-scoopers make the job less unpleasant.

scent at general nose level for other canines to smell and take notice.

This is a difficult problem to eradicate because, unlike other house-training problems, it is instinctive. Using a water pistol to squirt your dog in the face as you command "No" each time you catch him may discourage him. However, it will not stop him carrying out the action in your absence nor remove the cause. Commercial deterrent sprays applied to his favorite sites may help, but you will need to keep spraying three or four times a day for a long time.

Castration appears to have the greatest chance of success because it reduces the need to mark territory. So a visit to your local veterinarian for advice is worth considering.

Above: Puppies must learn the meaning of the command "No," but don't punish them when they make a mess in the house. Try to be tolerant until the puppy learns your house rules.

▶ Stopping Your Dog from Pulling

The bane of many people's lives are dogs—especially large ones—that drag them to and fro. A casual observer in any park is likely to see lots of dogs pulling their unwilling owners along. This book is concerned with behavioral problems rather than dog training, but I will refer to some dog-training methods here to help with dogs that pull on the lead. Next to not coming when called, heel training is the most common problem presented to a dog trainer or behavior practitioner. Amazingly, 95 percent of all dogs brought to me for pulling on the lead have attended a dog-training class. And most of them have been awarded a certificate of competence by the club even though the dogs pull. Work that one out!

In this chapter, I will introduce some training equipment that really does stop dogs pulling and that is quite simple to use. However, in the long term, you may need to receive one-to-one training from a professional trainer if you wish to have a dog that infallibly walks along with you without pulling.

The Language of Command

Few owners understand dog language, but even fewer dogs understand English. They do, however, learn to associate different voice tones with different situations, so commands should be delivered in a short, crisp voice. You may choose your own commands providing they are short, preferably just a single syllable. Praise must be given in a very soft tone of

Above: Be consistent and employ a firm tone of voice when teaching your dog basic commands. Praise in a softer voice so the dog can distinguish between the two.

voice (whispering is ideal—as we do with babies) for the dog to distinguish commands from praise. Equally, the dog should understand the word "No," and this should be delivered in a very

Even on a short lead, the dog is out of control.

sharp, commanding voice. Do not mumble or forget to use the same command for an exercise. In other words, make sure you know all the commands and are consistent with them before starting training.

Collar and Lead

For control, make sure you have the correct lead and collar. All puppies should be trained using a fixed collar and a lead about four to six feet (1.2–2 m) in length. Head halters, choke chains, and slip collars are not for use with puppies.

When trying to control adult dogs, many people buy a choke chain think-

❶

ing that somehow the dog will learn not to pull because the chain tightens on his neck when he does so. This is rarely the case, however, because a dog's natural gait is faster than ours and he cannot make the connection between the choking action of the chain and what you want him to do. I have used choke chains on certain dogs with good results—normally dogs for which all other training methods have failed. But it requires skill. I have yet to meet a person who can use a choke chain correctly without having a skilled trainer alongside. So don't think of using one on your own.

is consistently walked, but whether he is two feet (0.6 m) ahead of you or by your side is only important if you feel it is. That's why some dogs walked on a long lead that move slightly ahead of you do not seem inclined to pull any further. Of course, in town this

Already the owner is being pulled off balance.

③

Left 1, 2, and 3: This is turning into a walk on the wild side. The combination of a big, powerful dog that pulls on the lead can turn a pleasurable activity like a walk in the park into a nightmare. Such a dog is also liable to knock into other pedestrians.

Below: When heel training, it helps if your dog gets used to walking consistently on one side of you.

②

You may wonder why we have the dog on our left but hold the lead in our right hand. Simply, it leaves the left hand as a working tool nearest the dog. The right hand controls the lead. Although I teach my dogs to walk on my left and at my heel, it's not essential that all dogs walk in this position. In my view, it helps a dog to know on which side he

may not be conducive with busy pedestrian traffic.

Begin your heel training in a garden, a yard, a quiet part of the house, or any other quiet place with no distractions. Continue to practice there for the first few weeks, until you have reached a standard whereby the dog responds to your "Heel" and "Sit" commands.

Puppies and Less-Determined Pullers

When one trains a puppy on a lead and fixed collar (not a chain or slip collar), it quickly becomes clear that these little creatures are incredibly malleable and can learn to walk next to you in a matter of weeks providing there is enough motivation in your handling. This chapter is primarily concerned with adult or young adult dogs that already pull, but I will give some basic training information for puppies here because that's the ideal time to train a dog.

A puppy has no idea of what you want or why it is that walking on a lead and collar should not involve pulling. However, once a puppy has been habituated to the collar and lead in the home, we can begin heel work. I always use a cue link in all dog training, which means that I motivate the dog by some action that gives me her attention and then I give her a corresponding reward. In that way, pleasure is imparted to the puppy.

Walking to Heel

Holding a tidbit and/or a squeaky toy—puppies are easily distracted by our actions—I walk off commanding "Heel." When the puppy surges ahead of me, I turn to the right, simultaneously bending down with an outstretched left hand that is either holding a squeaking toy or offering a (very tiny) tasty treat. As the puppy takes a cue and follows my hand, I command "Heel" and give the tidbit or let the puppy mouth the toy. After repeating this action ten or more times, I throw the toy for the puppy, making a little game, and finish the exercise. I begin a new lesson later. The puppy has now begun to pay attention, is learning the command "Heel," and realizes that being beside me brings fun and rewards.

The next stage is to practice the heel exercises in different training locations, i.e., the street, park, and other public places. (Note: when near a road or on a public pavement, all exercises must be carried out on a lead—**no exceptions**.) At first the dog or puppy will be distracted; this is normal, so now you have to work harder. The dog may find the distractions more interesting than you, which is why this is often the time when a number of owners give up, because their dog appears to be regressing.

When walking to heel down a street, it is natural, when other dogs pass by, for your dog to display curiosity toward them. Don't stop—just carry on walking, praising your dog to bring her back to your side. At this point, you can offer a treat as a greater distraction to regain the dog's attention. Equally, you can snap check the lead on an adult dog if she stubbornly pulls toward them. Sometimes I start to run for about 15 feet (5 m), and most dogs find this exciting, wanting to follow me rather than pulling toward the other dog.

Stay in Control

Your dog must not be allowed to think that every time she sees another dog in the street or park she can stop listening to you. Obviously, you might wish your dog to play and socialize with other dogs as and when you choose. This is perfectly acceptable, as long as your dog is under your control at all times.

I use the same training methods for adult dogs but add another component. If the dog really surges ahead, I stop in my tracks, command the dog to sit, and do not move again until she calms down. Patience is required, perhaps over many weeks of training. If your dog lags behind you, under no circumstances pull her along, just use praise to encourage her back to your side.

Below 1, 2, and 3: When teaching puppies to walk to heel, a tidbit or toy can be used to encourage the puppy to follow your changes of direction. The dog is rewarded for following your commands, and the idea of staying by your side becomes attractive.

2

3

Heel Training— Recap

▶ "Heel" means a change of direction.

▶ Food and/or a toy presented to the dog connects the command to a reward.

▶ Throwing the toy adds another reward as does a swift, fun game at the end of the session.

Below: The appearance of another dog can cause your dog to strain at the lead in his eagerness to say hello. Don't let this habit become established as it will undo your good work. A snap check on the lead can be used with adult dogs to redirect their attention back to you.

Dog Training and Psychology Tips

▶ **1. Before you start to train your dog, make sure you fully understand the exercise you are about to teach. Do not attempt any exercise if you are in doubt.**

▶ **2. The motivation for your dog to learn is praise, delivered in a pleasant tone of voice. Very few puppies need physical correction—just patience and repetitive training with an enjoyable play period allowed at the end.**

▶ **3. You can be sure that if the dog appears to be making errors, the fault lies with the trainer who is not communicating clearly enough with the animal.**

▶ **4. When training, the dog may begin to lose interest or apparently understand and preempt your commands. Get him to perform an exercise he likes, praise him, finish training, and play a short game. Then try again later in the day.**

▶ **5. Remember that different breeds, bred with different working instincts, progress at different rates in training.**

▶ **6 Some dogs are compulsive sniffers. In this case, don't walk near walls or bushes, which harbor smells. Try and walk in the center of the pavement. This makes training easier.**

Using Head Halters with Determined Pullers

(for determined and dominant dogs only)
Head halters fit over the dog's foreface. They work well on most (but not all) dogs. I have found that determined or difficult dogs do settle down and learn not to pull.

Unfortunately, as they are are only made in about six sizes and dogs' faces vary in size greatly, they can sometimes rub, causing some minor irritation to the surface of the skin. Fitted properly, they are without doubt the best way to stop a skilled puller from stretch-

Left: Head halters should be used only with a strong and determined adult puller—they are not suitable for puppies and sensitive dogs. When used properly, they can achieve excellent results.

ing your arms. Once adopted, most dogs walk alongside you and their head halter remains loose.

How to Fit a Head Halter onto a Dog

It's very important to introduce the head halter to your dog slowly and to let the dog develop good associations with wearing it. Most people rush the introduction and then become upset at their dog's stressed reaction to it. Avoid this by following my advice.

First, get your dog to sit with a lead and collar on. Have several juicy tidbits at hand. Then place the head halter on your dog and reward him with a tidbit. Leave the head halter on your dog for a few minutes; give a food reward intermittently. Your dog should now associate having the head halter fitted with receiving a reward. This needs to be repeated three times daily for about ten minutes duration each time over a period of three days. Next, attach the lead to the head halter, and walk your dog a short distance in the house or yard; reward your dog at short intervals. If your dog panics or attempts to rub his head on the floor (which is normal), distract him with the food and use your lead to make him sit.

Most dogs resent the head halter at first but quickly adapt as they come to associate it with food rewards and walks. Once you can walk your dog without adverse reaction around the house or yard, you're ready for normal outdoor use. Do persevere, and don't give up or feel sorry for your dog. Otherwise you'll be back to square one.

Using a Body Harness

(for determined and dominant dogs only)

There are also special harnesses to help stop dogs pulling. This is a device that uses thin cord that passes under the dog's front legs (armpits). When the dog surges ahead, the cords pull tight

Below, left, and right: A dog needs to become accustomed to wearing a face collar—food rewards are useful during the introductory period.

on the dog's "armpits," causing discomfort. When the dog stops pulling, there is no discomfort. The dog dictates the comfort measure he experiences, and in this way many dogs quickly learn to stop pulling. Like the head halter, it is a simple, straightforward training aid that works well.

> ## Recap
>
> - With puppies and less determined adult dogs, practice heel training using rewards to reinforce good behavior.
>
> - Determined and strong adult dogs can be trained by the intelligent use of head halters or body harnesses.

▶Introducing a New Dog into the Family

Introducing a new dog into the family is usually a smooth operation with few major incidents. However, the ease with which a new dog settles in depends on several factors. Any dogs living with you—even if it's only one—view themselves as being in a pack with a set hierarchy. So any newcomer will be regarded as competition and will be watched carefully. Some dogs will just consider a newcomer a nuisance while others may become aggressive and try to intimidate the perceived threat. How your dog reacts depends on her dominance levels and/or relationship with you.

To start with, we need to understand what goes through your dog's mind and through the mind of the new arrival. If the new dog is a puppy, then this will present different problems and will require an alternative introduction method. The sex of any resident dogs and of the new arrival (excluding puppies) will also play a significant role in how smoothly the first few days go.

Above: Jealousies can arise when a resident dog has to share her home with a newcomer. The status quo of the pack hierarchy is being challenged.

A New Puppy

I always purchase an indoor pen and sometimes a cage for a new puppy. This allows the puppy freedom while the resi-dent dog can enjoy some peace. Also, like a child's playpen, it is a place where a new puppy can be placed out of harm's way when the household is very busy.

When the puppy arrives, the resident dog will be most inquisitive or even a little aggressive to the newcomer depending on how well socialized the resident dog is. Place the puppy in the pen, and allow the resident dog into the room so they can sniff one another through the bars and become acquainted. I never leave a puppy alone with a resident dog for the first three weeks and after that only if I am sure they do get on well. Resident dogs should always be able to get away from a puppy when they want to—this alone will prevent most confrontations in the early stages of introduction. If you do experience aggression from the resi-dent dog, read the section on inter-pack aggression (Chapter 11) to understand the dynamics of the situation more clearly.

A new puppy will slowly adjust to his new environment; he will view any resident dog as a playmate and friend whether this is appreciated or not. Adult dogs seem to know instinctively that pups are trouble and tend to growl when approached or jumped upon, especially if this playfulness is accompanied by sharp teeth. The resident dog may growl as a warning to the puppy if he's being annoying, and even the odd bite should be allowed because it is given more as a warning than an act of aggression. If possible, leave the dogs to sort themselves out without your interference.

Below 1, 2, and 3: When any new dog is introduced to a household, he is bound to be inquisitive and want to investigate his surroundings. You should allow this, but also be aware that a resident dog will need her own space.

①

②

③

After about a week or so, the new puppy will generally be tolerated, and in time it may even become liked.

The puppy will want to play with the resident dog and will soon become attached to her and learn from her. So if your resident dog has any bad habits, like being aggressive to other dogs or jumping up on people, try to avoid the pup copying these from the beginning. If possible, gently obedience train the puppy from six weeks of age, keeping him away from the older dog during lessons; also walk the puppy on his own once or twice a week, and concentrate on the puppy's obedience.

Maintain Pack Position

A common problem when a second or third dog arrives is that owners lose control when the puppy becomes too attached to the resident dog. You must keep control. Though it's necessary for the dogs to develop a healthy relationship, it should not be at the expense of your being accepted as pack leader.

Enroll in puppy socialization classes when possible. Because of vaccination requirements, you won't be able to take your dog when he is very young, but you can use this time to read about training and perhaps visit the different classes in your area to watch and learn. Then when you do bring your puppy, you'll already be acquainted with other members' dogs and you'll have judged which is the best class for you and your dog.

Left: He looks adorable to us, but a resident dog will view him quite differently. In general, you should try to allow the two to establish their respective pack positions without undue interference.

Below 1: It is sensible to use an indoor training cage when introducing a puppy to a dog.

Below 2 and 3: The two animals will be able to sniff and get to know one another through the bars without there being any danger of aggression from the older dog.

Do's and Don'ts with a New Puppy

At the beginning, **don't** leave the new puppy unattended with the resident dog (unless the puppy is in an indoor training cage).

Do ensure the resident dog has somewhere to escape to away from the puppy if she so chooses.

Do consider buying an indoor pen or cage for a new puppy, especially if he shows signs of overboisterousness; the cage also allows for short spells of peace and helps in toilet training.

If the adult dog reprimands the puppy, **don't** intervene unless the adult dog will not let go or continues biting as opposed to administering a snap, a single bite, or a growl. They will sort themselves out.

Don't pay too much attention to the puppy at the expense of the resident dog. When the two approach you for greeting, always show preference for the resident dog first (not equal affection)—otherwise jealousies may occur.

If the breeds are of very different sizes, for example the resident is a Yorkie and the new dog is a Labrador puppy, **do** try to avoid bullying by the puppy. Use obedience control if the smaller resident dog cannot defend herself.

Do feed the dogs separately for the first weeks, and then, if the resident dog doesn't seem to mind, slowly bring their bowls nearer while encouraging good manners.

Don't allow the puppy or adult dog to gobble all the food. The resident dog has the right to growl or bite the puppy if he tries to take her food. Sometimes he will learn from this warning, sometimes not.

If the family children wish to play with the puppy—as they normally do—then do make sure it's done in another part of the house or yard so as not to create jealousies. This is especially important in the first few weeks. Remember to tell the children to show more affection to the resident dog when both dogs are present.

Introducing Adults of the Opposite Sex

(Two handlers are required during socialization)

Warning: If a fight breaks out when the new dog and the resident dog meet for the first time (this is especially likely if it occurs on one or the other's home territory), then this can be a very serious setback to future harmony. First impressions are important to dogs, so avoid this circumstance if possible.

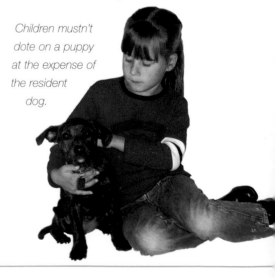

Children mustn't dote on a puppy at the expense of the resident dog.

If you haven't chosen the new dog yet, then do take time to select a dog that is different from your resident dog in sex, temperament, and size. If you choose dogs that are similar in terms of temperament and strength, you could be courting trouble in the future. If you introduce dogs of the opposite sex to each other on neutral territory, this makes life a lot easier—though some dogs will not even entertain a new friend on these terms. Have the dogs on leads, and try to introduce them on a walk. If this goes well, then release them; if they play, that's a good sign.

Getting Acquainted

If there is no obvious aggression, then the next step is to allow both dogs to meet in your yard and eventually in the home. One dog may be dominant and one may be submissive: don't be distressed if one dog appears to dominate the other—it's their way of sorting out who's boss.

If either dog displays aggression (by biting or attacking), then on their next meeting they should be kept on leads and both dogs should be given a food reward as they come into sight of each other. This should build up a good association with meeting. Repeat such meetings and food rewards until a good rapport is established.

Don't play any ball games or games that involve competition between the dogs: this could create friction and cause possessive or dominant aggression.

When the dogs have fully accepted each other, normal retrieve games can be introduced if no problems are encountered. As with puppies, always show the resident dog preferential treatment when both dogs approach you for praise or greeting—don't think you can treat them equally. Also bear in mind that the new dog may eventually become the dominant dog and preferential treatment will then have to be given to him whether you like it or not. The dogs should be fed separately until you have established their compatibility and tolerance of one another during feeding.

Above: Always greet a resident dog first and show her preference while she remains at the top of the dogs' pack hierarchy.

Below: Feeding time can be the occasion for displays of aggression if one dog tries to muscle in on the other's bowl. Feed dogs separately until you have seen that they are getting on and will tolerate one another's presence.

Introducing Adults of the Same Sex

If the adult dogs are of the same sex, then they must be socialized before they start to live together unless you have a very submissive resident or new arrival. Do this as described in the previous section. There is definitely more chance of fighting for pack position and rivalry between dogs of the same sex, and when it happens the fights can be terrible.

Don't leave any new adults alone with each other in case of fighting. If the dogs are going to get along, then after an initial week or two of mutual appraisal, they will begin to relate and play with one another or show affection. They may just ignore one another, but that's quite unusual. The governing factors are how dominant the dogs are by temperament and how you treat the dogs during the initial weeks of acclimatization. On balance, it is a hit-and-miss affair with dogs of the same sex, just like humans.

If the resident or new dog seems overprotective of toys and bones, then remove them from the home. If the new dog is insecure and needs extra reassurance, then make sure that you have periods alone with him at first; this stops the resident dog becoming jealous of him. Out of sight, out of mind.

Above: Take care when introducing dogs of the same sex—apparently playful behavior can change and violent fights may break out between them quite suddenly.

Left: It may take some time for dogs to become accustomed to one another, but eventually most dogs will settle down and happily accept one another's company. Many even become good friends.

Don't create too much excitement when it's time for a walk or when visitors arrive; any sudden excitement can trigger excitement in the dogs, causing one to snap at the other. It can also cause the dogs to try to dominate the situation by getting the first greeting from the visitor. Be watchful for any strange behavior like staring at each other or constant avoidance of one another. Even after many weeks, the occasional growl, lack of play between the dogs, or one dog seeming to be constantly fearful can be signs that things are not working.

▶ Introducing Adult Dogs — Recap

▶ **Try to choose a dog different in size, sex, and temperament from the resident dog.**

▶ **Initially introduce the dogs to one another on leads on neutral territory.**

▶ **Use rewards to help develop a good association in the dogs' minds with meeting one another.**

▶ **Avoid competitive games.**

▶ **Show the resident dog preferential treatment at first when the two dogs are together, but be prepared to change if the pack order changes.**

Tug-of-war games can turn into assertions of dominance.

It would be advisable here to remove the toy.

Above: Competitive games that encourage the dogs to pit themselves against one another should be avoided. It is also advisable to choose dogs that are dissimilar in size, sex, and temperament when you decide to introduce a new dog to a resident dog that is already part of the household.

In Conclusion

Only dogs can decide whether they like each other, irrespective of what we may feel. But we can help to prepare the best environment for that to happen. Don't force two dogs together who are obviously incompatible. Happily, 90 percent of adult dogs and puppies do eventually sort out their position and status within the family pack and learn to live together with little fuss or trouble.

Phobias and Fears

A phobia is an abnormal and irrational fear of something. Dogs can suffer from phobias just like people, and like people they need help to overcome them. Of course, humans who wish to tackle a phobia can discuss the irrationality of their fears with a therapist. Dogs can't, but communication on some level is essential. Phobic animals are among the most difficult cases presented to a behavior practitioner. Essentially, the approach is to create a situation in which the animal's desire to obtain a reward outweighs his fear.

Signs of Phobic Fear

- **Leaping into owner's arms**
- **Hiding**
- **Shaking**
- **Growling**
- **Urination and defecation**
- **Bulging eyes**
- **Salivating**
- **Panting**
- **Bolting**

1, 2, 3, and 4: These are some of the physical signs of a phobic reaction. A dog may have bulging eyes (1), growl (2), start shaking (3), or hide and cower (4) in an attempt to get away from the cause of the fear.

What Causes Phobias?

Some dogs simply inherit a predisposition to fearfulness. Fears that are apparent at a very young age, prior to 12 weeks, may well have been inherited unless there has been a very obvious bad experience during that early period. Such inborn fears are almost impossible to cure, which is why gundog trainers usually give up on pups that are "gun-shy" (sound phobic of gunfire without apparent cause).

However, in my experience, most phobias are caused by a traumatic experience. In some cases, this can be so minor that the owner was unaware of it. For example, the seeds of a full-blown phobia might be sown when a dog is alarmed by the owner casually turning on a food mixer or shaking out a plastic trash bag. In other cases, the original frightening experience can be identified—a crack of thunder, a fireworks display, low-flying aircraft, or simply a black plastic bag flying down the street.

Prevention by Socialization

The best safeguard against the development of phobias is socialization for puppies between six and 12 weeks. It is at this age that your dog needs to be introduced to a wide range of environmental and social experiences to enable him to develop into a well-adjusted adult. However, it is also at this age that puppies are most acutely susceptible to developing fears. So it's vital at this stage to think about this bewildering new world from a dog's point of view. For example, if you walk behind a parked car with the engine running, you might be startled when exhaust fumes hit your legs. Now imagine being a dog in this situation. His head is at exhaust height, so the fumes will blast straight into his face. This is much more frightening, and of course the dog cannot understand what has happened as we can. Most dogs, like people, will adjust and shrug it off. Others, quite understandably, may develop a phobia related to the back of cars.

The Wild Animal in a Dog

Wild dogs and wolves can deal with frightening experiences by running away. Their territory is vast, and any threat (real or perceived) can be left miles behind. Domestic dogs have the same inbuilt reaction to frightening experiences but often cannot deal with fear in the way their instincts tell them to. We constrain them with doors, walls, fences, roadways, and leads. Denied the flight option, puppies need to develop the confidence to cope with an unnatural environment.

Many dogs are frightened of sudden loud bangs—fireworks, thunder, gunshots or automatic bird scarers. On a lead, they may become hysterical with fear; off lead, they may bolt. The fear may even extend to apprehension of being in the area where the sound was first heard. Surprisingly, even dogs that have accepted loud noises for years may develop noise phobia later in life.

Above: By playing tape recordings of loud noises at low volume to dogs that have a phobia about noise, slowly the dog can be desensitized to the cause of her fear.

Certain breeds and certain strains within breeds also appear to inherit a predisposition to this type of phobia.

Beating the Bangs

First of all, make a clean start. Don't force your dog back to the area that he already associates with the frightening noise. Once the association is fixed in the dog's mind, it is almost impossible to break. I call this location fear.

Introduce a new regimen by buying prerecorded sounds of thunder and loud bangs for a desensitization program. Using a small tape recorder, play one of the sounds at a level (very low) that does not cause panic in the dog. It may cause some fear, but low-key reaction is fine. Whenever you do this, at the same time provide a positive distraction from the fear sound being played. For example:
• Offer food rewards in the form of favorite treats. (Make sure the dog is very hungry beforehand.)
• Start an exciting game with a toy.

Ignore any negative behavioral response, i.e., if the dog shows fear, don't reassure or pat him but demonstrate by your own behavior that nothing frightening is happening.

If you are carrying out this exercise outdoors, use a retractable lead to ensure that your dog cannot bolt. If you can persuade a friend to help, one of you can walk the dog on lead while the other walks a parallel route some 20 yards (18 m) away, playing the tape recording—at a very low level to begin with. Over time, decrease the distance and/or increase the volume gradually. It may take many months and dozens of practice sessions, but that is the only way to make progress.

Left: You should avoid petting a dog that shows signs of phobia—act as if there is nothing to worry about.

the treat being heightened by reserving the ball or other retrieve toy for desensitization sessions only. I have found that most will go for the ball, providing the audio sounds are moderate in level.

Household Noises

Some dogs develop phobias about certain household noises, such as wine corks popping or even sheets of aluminum foil rustling. In such cases, try combining the particular sound with your dog's mealtime. While you prepare the food, start making the problem noise—as quietly as you can. Then quickly get a helper to place your dog's food on the floor well away from the noise area, maybe in the next room.

The dog now has a choice to make: panic or eat. At first he may be hesitant, but if he goes for the food, however cautiously, you are on the way to success. If he ignores the food and flees, take up the food bowl and try again later in the day or even next day, when hunger will be on your side. (This method won't work if you feed tidbits at other times—food must be linked only with the key noise.)

Do what you can to calm the dog without adding to his panic. If he needs a dark room, let him have it. If he wants to lean

If there is any particular game or situation that really excites your dog, then use that as a distraction to the recorded sound and see which wins the day. For example, you can offer fanatical retrievers a choice between playing a retrieve game or giving in to the fear,

Right: If your dog develops a phobia about a household noise, you can try preparing her food at the same time as the noise is being produced. Often the dog will perk up at the thought of food and will dig into her bowl rather than fleeing the room in fright.

> ## ▶ Beating Fear Reactions—Recap
>
> ▶ **Use tape recordings initially at a very low level and/or at a good distance from the dog.**
>
> ▶ **Don't reward a fear reaction by offering comfort.**
>
> ▶ **Use a retractable lead to stop the dog bolting.**
>
> ▶ **Provide positive distractions—food or play.**

Below 1 and 2: Food can also be used as a way of encouraging a dog to accept the presence of an object that normally would induce an attack of panic. Gradually reduce the distance between the two as the dog is eating. It is likely to be a slow process, but over time the dog should learn that the object does not pose a real threat.

❶ **❷**

against your leg or follow you from room to room, accept this. But don't comfort him, either verbally or by petting him, because that will only confirm his sense that there is something to be scared of. A matter-of-fact attitude on your part gives him much more real reassurance.

Taping the Trouble

If your dog is afraid of a specific noise—a vacuum cleaner, motorbike, etc.—a tape recorder can again help. Record the noise in question. Pick a time when there is a pleasant distraction for your dog, like a fun game or a meal, and play back the noise at a very low volume for ten minutes. Repeat this exercise three times a day for ten weeks. When your dog is comfortable with the sound, raise the volume slightly, gradually working toward the normal level that the dog would encounter in reality. This method has a good success record.

Fear of Objects

If your dog fears specific objects, such as cars, vacuum cleaners, animals, children, or people in general, then get him to confront these fears at a distance he can tolerate. When he remains calm, reward him on the spot with a tidbit or a portion of his daily dinner. Gradually reduce the distance and continue to reward your dog with tidbits. It also helps to try to vary the circumstances, as this can help to build up a pleasant association with the problem.

Slow introduction many times a week over a long period of time has the best chance of success. Do not force your dog, shout at him, or threaten him at any time if he becomes frightened. Equally, never praise or reward him while he is displaying signs of fear but only when he relaxes.

▶ Tranquilizers

▶ Tranquilizers can be used for one-time affairs like fireworks night, but please first seek your veterinarian's advice. Such drugs should be used only on a temporary basis and not permanently or over long periods.

▶ General Tips

▶ **Never force a frightened dog to go near to the source of his fear.**

▶ **Don't bend down and cuddle a frightened dog—this only makes matters worse.**

▶ **Ignoring the dog's fear demonstrates that you know there is nothing to worry about.**

▶ **If the dog is scared of something you can easily avoid, then avoid it!**

▶ **Long-term use of tranquilizers is not a solution.**

▶ **Some dogs are reassured by the company of other, more confident dogs. Try borrowing a calm dog from a friend.**

▶ **Always ensure that your dog has a strong lead and secure collar so that if panic sets in, he cannot bolt.**

▶ Car Sickness

Some dogs become carsick in the same way that people do. They feel queasy and may even throw up. Dogs can also drool profusely and may appear soaking wet at the end of a short trip because of salivation caused by the journey. Some dogs learn to anticipate a car journey, reacting to cues like the car keys being taken out by the owner or the car doors being opened. These dogs may start to drool prodigiously even before they have been put in the vehicle. Other dogs can shake with fear—these are all symptoms of car sickness in its various forms.

Above and left: *Try to accustom a dog to car travel so that he comes to associate it with fun activities, like walks in the park. Then the jangle of your car keys will be greeted with eager anticipation.*

Causes

Most dogs love traveling by car because they like the proximity of people that they experience in a car and they know that often they are going somewhere exciting, like a park. However, some dogs find the experience upsetting. This is caused by a combination of the disconcerting motion and the lurching of the car under braking and subsequent acceleration. The usual symptoms of car sickness are excessive drooling, a dull facial appearance, and, in more serious cases, actual vomiting and diarrhea.

▶ Prevention Advice

From the start, accustom your dog to car travel. This can take place as early as six weeks when the chances of forming positive associations with the car are highest. When the puppy has an empty stomach, take him for short trips lasting no longer than five minutes. If these trips are frequent, they will quickly create a positive attitude, and your dog will associate car travel with the rewards of attention, companionship, and—when he is old enough—shopping and walks in the park. These end rewards are what make dogs love the car.

For puppies and older dogs who have already reacted badly to car journeys, we need a strategy to make car travel more attractive. Try this plan of action that can be modified according to your circumstances.

Week 1 During this week, don't take your dog for a ride in the car. Cover the seat or, in a van or wagon, the floor with an old blanket for security and warmth. Begin feeding your dog at least two meals a day in the car. At first, you may sit alongside the dog and then after a few days, if all is well, close the door with the dog inside for a few minutes. For the first few meals, allow your dog to jump in and out when finished. The food, if the dog is hungry, should motivate him to investigate the car. After that, shut your dog in the car for five minutes at each meal time, making sure you leave the windows ajar for ventilation. When you let him out, make no fuss; behave as if it's no great feat but a part of his routine. If the dog does not drool or show discomfort, then you are ready for stage two.

Week 2 Continue as with week 1, but now introduce five-minute drives at least twice daily after the dog has finished eating. Five minutes is not long enough for most dogs to start feeling sick. When the dog has reached a stage where he no longer seems uncomfortable, we are ready for stage three.

Week 3 Take your dog by car to the park each day, providing the journey isn't more than 15 minutes from your home. Exercise him and then return home. You can place chews or tidbits in the car for him on the journey. Give no tidbits of food at any other time of the day.

By lengthening journey times, you can make further progress until the desired result is achieved. This system works really well as long you don't try to rush the training—patience really is required.

Further Tips

• If practical, buy a seat harness that attaches to a seat belt. You can use this to strap your dog in the rear seat, and this sometimes helps to reduce the rocking motion that can cause nausea.

• Avoid journeys in heavy traffic, as endless stopping and starting serves only to exacerbate the problem.

• During the daytime, occasionally put your dog in the car for ten minutes or so. Then simply let your dog out of the car without any fuss. In this way, your dog won't always anticipate a car journey, and this should reduce his anticipatory sickness.

• Don't take your dog on long journeys until he can consistently manage short ones.

• If your dog is extremely frightened of travel, then travel sickness pills may help, but in the long term they will not change the feelings the dog associates with the car for the better. Consult your veterinarian for advice.

Above: *This dog is ready to ride. When car journeys lead to pleasant experiences, dogs are keen to get inside.*

Above and right: *The nausea that dogs experience in a car may be caused by motion sickness. In such cases, it can help to secure the dog to a seat belt with a seat harness like this (above). Also periods spent in a stationary car (right) help a dog to lose her anticipatory fear of getting into the vehicle.*

Digging Up the Garden

As far as dogs are concerned, digging is a perfectly normal activity. Perhaps they have found an interesting smell or they want to bury a bone for a rainy day. On hot days, they may be trying to find cooler soil to lie on. For some dogs, it's an outlet to relieve boredom or anxiety, while for many it's just an enjoyable activity. So though it often appears destructive and pointless to us, it's as natural to a dog as yawning is to his owner.

Prevention Advice

If the digging is as a symptom of boredom or anxiety, then the dog is possibly being left alone for too long and the digging is a type of relief mechanism for the dog. Make sure that the dog is receiving adequate exercise and stimulation. Possibly giving your dog more attention by playing games with him will be all that's needed to make him content and stop him digging.

If your dog digs solely in one place or digs up specific shrubs, then place a large stone slab in the hole and cover it with a few inches of soil or turf. Alternatively,

place slabs on the surface around the base of the shrub. This takes the fun out of digging for all but the keenest dog.

If you're experiencing digging for the first time with a new puppy or adult dog, then the simplest solution may be to fence off the part of the garden you wish to protect. Another possibility is an outdoor kennel and pen. This will keep a puppy out of mischief until he matures and provides a permanent solution for the persistent adult digger.

Directing digging to an acceptable area is easier than trying to stop it. Confine your dog to part of the yard designated for digging by fencing him in it or tethering him there for short periods. When your dog tries to dig elsewhere, take him to his digging area and leave him. Be sure he can't get tangled and has shade, water, and other diversions. Don't leave him unsupervised.

A better way is to give your dog the ultimate digging spot. Just as a child digs in a sandbox, your dog can be enticed to dig in a doggy sandbox. Mark a clearly defined area, and fill it with sand. Then spike the area by burying your dog's favorite treats and toys. Continue to bait the area every day until your dog learns that digging there is rewarding compared with the rest of the yard. Keep up the habit by occasionally planting buried treasures.

Above: One tactic to thwart a persistent digger is to restrict his movements to an outdoor pen that is provided with a kennel.

Training Disks

Direct action to stop digging tends to be difficult to enforce as it is often hard to catch the dog at the moment when he is committing the offense. However, on occasions it can work. Teach your dog indoors to associate the sound of train-

❶

them; this stimulates their canine curiosity. One remedy for this sort of behavior is to spray bitter apple, which is quite repugnant to dogs, around the base of the valuable plants. As an alternative, antimate spray can be used, though in both cases rain will wash them away, so reapply the spray after rain.

ing disks with your commands. When your dog is fully conditioned to respond to the sound that the disks make when shaken in your hand, then this reaction can be transposed outdoors. When you see your dog about to dig, rattle the disks. Most dogs stop immediately upon hearing the sound, provided early conditioning has been taught properly.

Another method is to allow your dog into the garden when you are present. Keep the training disks or a large bunch of old keys in your pocket. If you see your dog digging, throw the keys just behind him and command "No" simultaneously. This will distract your dog from digging; when he looks up, call him to you in a kind voice and praise him when he comes. It's important to carry out this method without the dog seeing your action. In this way, he may come to associate the command "No" and the clattering noise with digging, and this will discourage the behavior.

❷

Deterrents—Recap

▸ • **Use the sound of rattled training discs to discourage a dog from digging if he has learned to associate the sound with stopping an action.**

▸ • **Spray bitter-smelling scent around the base of plants.**

▸ • **Repeat the application of spray after rain.**

Scent Deterrents

Many dogs that chew newly planted shrubs and plants repeatedly do so because they can smell human scent on

❸

Above 3: Spraying a bitter-tasting spray around the base of a plant usually deters a dog from digging it up. Remember to reapply the spray after rain.

Eating Animal Feces

Dogs seem to have a natural desire to eat the excrement of herbivorous animals—cattle, sheep, and horse dung being the favorites. It seems a disgusting habit to us, especially when you know that the same dog will probably jump up at you next to give you a big lick as an enthusiastic greeting. Cat litter trays are something else that some dogs seek out for a quick snack. This is a particularly distasteful habit to many people. In this case, I purchase a covered litter tray (with a hood on it) and make the entrance just big enough for the cat to pass through.

In reality, eating feces is quite normal. As far as your dog is concerned, this is a dietary supplement to meat and she is only following her instincts. This is especially true of puppies and adolescent dogs who are still learning what to eat—they are very curious and eager to explore a new world.

Above: "I'm pleased to see you, but what were you eating a moment ago?" Dogs that eat feces repel us, even though the habit is quite natural to them.

Dietary deficiency is often suggested as a reason for this behavior, but this is not borne out by my experience. The dogs I've personally seen are in the prime of health and eat a well-balanced diet. Whatever the cause, the effect produced in you the owner is uniformly simple: revulsion! Unfortunately, it's not always an easy habit to break. However, you should persist because parasitic infestation from whatever fecal matter your dog consumes can be a problem.

Prevention Advice

Dogs That Eat Their Own Feces

The obvious prevention method in this case is to clean up after your dog has defecated. You can make life easier by feeding the animal natural food. Dry foods on the whole produce more fecal matter, so changing your dog's food to a high-quality meat-based diet will

Below: A dog that eats her own feces may be showing signs of boredom. In such cases, ensure that the dog receives plenty of stimulation in the form of toys, play, and the pleasures of human company.

reduce her output. Tripe especially produces dark, almost black feces that dogs seem to find less palatable. Feeding once daily will also help to reduce the number of times your dog defecates.

I believe the most common reason why puppies and young dogs begin to explore their own feces is boredom. Dogs left alone in an unstimulating environment learn to eat feces especially when the feces are left for long periods in their presence. This early conditioning is very powerful and the answer is clear. Avoid these circumstances, and from an early age, give your dog a stimulating lifestyle with chew toys to play with and plenty of interaction with you and other animals.

Dogs Eating Feces of Other Animals

Herbivores' feces are very attractive to many dogs who view it as a supplement to their diet. Wolves have no problem with digesting copious amounts of elk, deer, and other animal feces that complements their nutri-

Left: Even the kitten looks shocked! Cat litter trays prove tempting fare for some dogs, but the answer is simple—fit the tray with a hood.

The collars that contain a remotely controlled jet spray that are described in the section on training aids provide an excellent way of intercepting your dog as she is about to eat any unpleasant matter. The spray is nontoxic and very effective. The spray collar works by filling the air around your dog's nose with a pungent-smelling vapor that soon makes the target feces less attractive. When properly timed, this deterrent method has a startling and positive effect—but you must be taught how to use it properly by a trainer.

tional needs. They cannot digest vegetation as thoroughly as herbivorous animals can, and so eating partly digested matter is a way of getting the nutrition required. For dogs that eat other dogs' feces, a number of manufacturers offer preparations that you can mix with their food (they contain sulfur). This apparently has a foul taste in expelled feces, making it less palatable. However, the results are no better than average if you are dealing with a determined feces eater.

Line Training

If you are out walking in places where the dog is likely to indulge this habit, then attach a 30-foot (9-m) nylon line to her collar. While the line is attached, don't let your dog play with other dogs as the line will tangle. When your dog attempts to eat feces, jerk sharply on the line and command "No" at the same time. This can have an effect if the dog is checked consistently in this fashion. Praise her when she returns to you.

Redirect Your Dog's Attention

The success of this method relies on your dog having a favorite ball or toy that she has learned to fetch on command. Now when your dog is about to go near or eat feces, call her name and command "Fetch" as you throw the ball. As the dog returns to you, run backward and praise her when she reaches you. In this way, you use play as a means to interrupt the behavior.

Deterrent Methods

Though not always pleasant to the eye, using a cage-type face muzzle is the only sure way of preventing your dog from eating feces and stopping her getting the repetitive reward of doing so, which reinforces the habit. I prefer to use this method as a starter for the first month as it is 100 percent effective in stopping the bad habit. When you come to stop using the muzzle, then some of the other methods can be considered.

Above: Dogs that will not respond to corrective training may have to be fitted with muzzles. It's not a pretty solution, but it's certainly effective.

▶Chasing People and Animals

Chasing animals is one of the strongest natural instincts in dogs. Pursuit and hunting behavior is as natural to a dog as walking is to a human. It is an expression of the desire to chase prey. Dominant as well as fear-driven dogs may exhibit predatory aggressive behavior that involves chasing. They go through the motions but don't usually attack or bite at the end of the chase, although this can change as such dogs get more practiced at it. If your dog chases other animals or dogs aggressively, refer to the section about dog-on-dog aggression.

The habit normally gets out of control when the dog begins to chase other animals or people persistently. Each successful chase, which is rewarded by the sight of the other animal or jogger trying to escape, encourages the dog to do it again. However, if caught in the early stages, you have a good chance of nipping it in the bud and stopping the habit altogether.

Sizing Up the Problem

Identify the problem as early as possible. Excitable dogs like Border Collies and terriers often become chase dogs because their owners ignorantly allow them as puppies to chase rabbits and squirrels in the local park, not realizing that they may be setting the stage for more serious behavior problems later on. Behavior that it practiced over several months becomes an embedded habit.

Some dogs often become bored when out for a walk with their owner. They start to seek stimulation in other animals and people, usually beginning with anything that is moving quickly away from them. With repetition, this behavior becomes reinforced and the problem becomes harder to

correct. Joggers in the local park are easy targets because they always seem to run off at pace when the dog decides to bark and/or give chase. If the jogger were to turn and give the dog a nasty fright, the dog would soon find pursuit less attractive. Unfortunately, this rarely happens. The end result is that a large number of dogs develop even worse habits, such as biting and serious aggression toward other people.

Obedience Training

Obedience training is the best corrective method to try first. Consult a qualified trainer, and train your dog in the environment where the problem arises. The "Recall" and the "Down-Stay" commands given at a distance are particularly useful with this

problem and should be taught thoroughly. With time, you should begin to attain some dominance over the dog. Also check the section on long-line training in the Recall chapter in this book (see Chapter 4). This enables you to gain control over your dog when she is some distance away from you

Reverse Chase

(for dogs that chase only people)
Ask a friend whom the dog doesn't know to jog in an area where you habitually walk. Equip your friend with a clean plastic bottle full of water or a water pistol. If your dog pursues this jogger, then you should jet water in the dog's face. Alternatively, use a dog stop alarm (see the section on training

Above: We all expect dogs to chase cats, but the behavior gets problematic when the targets are people, horses, other dogs, or livestock. If the dog goes uncorrected, the habit will get progressively worse.

aids) or a loud football rattle; these can be activated near the pursuing dog. If the dog has been preconditioned to the sound of training disks, a set of disks can be thrown at the dog's feet while she is in pursuit. From the dog's point of view, the pursuit is no longer rewarded by a pleasurable experience, and this often is enough to cause the behavior to cease.

Redirecting the Chase

Dogs like chasing things, and probably the most popular toy is a ball.

Distraction training works with some dogs, especially those that love retrieving. Teach the dog to retrieve to a competent level. Do not play any retrieve games with your dog except when you are out in the areas where the chase is likely to occur. The aim is to transfer your dog's attention from the chase to the retrieve, so timing is vital. You must focus the dog's attention on the retrieve just as she is starting to think of chasing something, not after the chase has begun. Then, at the correct time, throw the ball and reward your dog with verbal and physical praise when she returns.

Electric Collars

A spray collar combined with recall training can also be helpful. However, in very serious cases where an attack may may be committed, I will use an electric shock collar. It might be appropriate, for example, when a dog chases people or livestock aggressively. However, a word of warning, you **must** have training first before attempting to use one. Wrongly used, they can traumatize the dog. **Never** buy an electric collar and hope to learn on your dog. See a canine behaviorist or a very competent dog trainer. And make sure you have tried and exhausted all the other training techniques I have outlined first.

Right: If your dog loves chasing balls and you can get your timing right, it's possible to redirect his attention away from the intended target of his pursuit to a favorite ball thrown as a distraction.

Stopping Chasing—Recap

▷ **Identify the problem early, and try to correct it before the behavior becomes ingrained.**

▷ **Obedience train your dog to a high degree.**

▷ **Use a jet of water, dog stop alarm, or training disks to deter a dog when she is in hot pursuit.**

▷ **Use a ball to redirect your dog's urge to chase something onto another object**

▷ **Employ the dominance reduction program (see pages 44–47) to assert your authority.**

▷ **Check the recall training chapter, and practice the recall exercise.**

▷ **Consider using a muzzle if you dog tries to bite the target.**

►Index

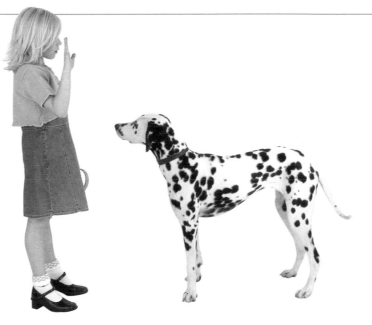

Author's Acknowledgments
I would like to say thank you to all the clients and friends who allowed me to photograph them and their dogs
for the purposes of this book. Special thanks also to:
Christopher Harvey for studio work; to Gist, Saphie and Lillie, my pets; to John France (canine behaviorist and trainer);
to Ross McCarthy (canine behaviorist and trainer);
to John Bowe for his technical assistance; to Karl Holt for production and technical advice;
and to John Ashford; Stephen, Juliet and Gabriella; Kelly Brown; Charlie Brown; Libby Grey;
and Mike Turner, my writing advisor.

A big vote of appreciation to Philip and Malcolm for their tireless support and very adaptable skills
in helping me to construct such a complex work on dog behavior.

Picture Credits
Unless otherwise credited below, all the photographs reproduced in this book were taken by David Ward, Colin Tennant
and John Bowe in a studio established at Colin Tennant's Canine and Feline Behaviour Center in Hertfordshire.
Monty Sloan, Wolf Park: pages 16 top left (montage, right), 18–19 bottom center (montage, right),
19 top (montage, right). Neil Sutherland for Interpet: pages 172 bottom, 175 (both), 183 bottom,
196 top left, 196–197 top, 199 right.

Readers who seek more advice and information on
a broad range of topics concerning dog behavior and
training should visit Colin Tennant's website
(www.bowetennant.co.uk) where they will find
information about a series of instructional videos that
are available for purchase.